PARADISE

BELOW ZERO

T0321406

The Fesler-Lampert Minnesota Heritage Book Series

This series is published with the generous assistance of the John K. and Elsie Lampert Fesler Fund and David R. and Elizabeth P. Fesler. Its mission is to republish significant out-of-print books that contribute to our understanding and appreciation of Minnesota and the Upper Midwest.

PARADISE BELOW ZERO

The Classic Guide to Winter Camping

Calvin Rutstrum

Illustrated by Leslie Kouba

University of Minnesota Press
Minneapolis

Copyright 1968 by Calvin Rutstrum

Originally published in hardcover by The Macmillan Company, 1968.
Republished by arrangement with Scribner, an imprint of Simon &
Schuster, Inc.

All rights reserved. No part of this publication may be reproduced, stored in
a retrieval system, or transmitted, in any form or by any means, electronic,
mechanical, photocopying, recording, or otherwise, without the prior
written permission of the publisher.

First University of Minnesota Press edition, 2000

Published by the University of Minnesota Press
111 Third Avenue South, Suite 290
Minneapolis, MN 55401-2520
http://www.upress.umn.edu

A Cataloging-in-Publication record for this book is available from the
Library of Congress.

ISBN 978-0-8166-3682-2

The University of Minnesota is an equal-opportunity educator and employer.

23 22 21 20 19 18   10 9 8 7 6 5 4

ACKNOWLEDGMENTS

THE AUTHOR would like to thank the following:

Eddie Bauer Expedition Outfitter, 417 E. Pine, Seattle, Washington 98122, for the photos of the quilted-down undergarment, quilted-down parka with wolverine ruff, down halfbag, down sleeping unit, and winter canvas camp cot;

L. L. Bean Inc., Freeport, Maine 04032, for the photo of the duck pants;

Halvorson Equipment, Inc., 246 Lake Avenue South, Duluth, Minnesota 55802, for the photo of the large, enclosed, heated type Snowmobile;

Marble Arms Corp., Box 111, Gladstone, Michigan 49837, for the photos of the "Expert" pattern belt knife and the waterproof match safe;

Hudson's Bay Company, Northern Stores Department, Hudson's Bay House, Winnipeg 1, Manitoba, Canada, for the photo of the genuine Indian-made snowshoes;

Vermont Tubbs Products, Inc., Wallingford, Vermont 05773, for the photos of the Michigan and Bear Paw snowshoes, and the commercial type snowshoe lashing;

Taylor Instruments Companies, Consumer Products Division, Arden, North Carolina 28704, for the photo of the field thermometers;

Therm'x Corporation, Inc., 1268 Folsom Street, San Francisco, California 94103, for the photos of the catalytic type heaters.

Ron Winch, wildlife photographer, for the photo of the author.

TO MY WIFE,

Florence,

WHO DEFROSTED MANY

OF THE STIFFLY FROZEN SENTENCES

IN THIS MANUSCRIPT

CONTENTS

PARADISE

BELOW ZERO

CHAPTER

1

THE HUMAN COLD WEATHER EQUATION

ALONG the various arctic coasts, the first major snowfall produces a sense of exhilaration in every Eskimo village—a jubilation that strikes young and adult alike. This, we may be sure, is no mere caprice of mood prompted by the effects of weather. For the Eskimo, snow foretells a major change in his mode of living—a sudden heightening of seasonal interest, the beginning of travel by dog sled or motorized toboggan, the visiting of remote villages and outlying trading posts.

Increased mobility obviously does not provide the only advantages in the seasonal change. The very essentials of snow and ice themselves brighten the life of the Eskimo and expand his scope.

When we compare the Eskimo's response to winter in the arctic with the despairing attitude in metropolitan and rural areas of the Temperate Zone toward approaching winter, perhaps we need to examine rather critically the reaction to weather in general as it underlies our own overall mode of life. Most people, it seems, try to avoid winter by any means within their compass of existing economic and geographical circumstances. Seasonal migration of our human population to escape the cold has created a cultural change and exchange so vast it already involves a complicated overlap in state and federal legislation, affecting our tax structure, educational program—even a disturbance of our gold and currency. Physical and mental adjustment to cold and snow has become almost the indigenous, isolated exception.

The birth some winters ago of a baby in a Minneapolis, Minnesota, suburban snowdrift as a result of an auto accident that took place while the mother was en route to a hospital tends to point up the cold and snow fear complex. Newspaper reporters sought to give the story high, sensational human interest, until the receiving-room personnel of the hospital played it down as insignificant. The doctor receiving the mother and baby in his care stated that the baby could not have been born under more viable conditions—that many babies might have been saved had they been born in a fresh snowdrift rather than in the questionable asepsis of a modern home or hospital.

As a boy I experienced great exhilaration on the arrival of winter. After more than a half century, I have not lost it. While perhaps for wholesome acceptance of winter one needs a healthy, robust body that craves vigorous action and diversion from the too often physically enervating, comfortable norm, what seems the most important requirement of all is an understanding of the physiological relationship of mind and body as it adapts to the little-understood exigencies of cold and snow.

At this writing, in an outer Minneapolis-St. Paul suburb on the St. Croix River, I am looking through an array of picture windows on the heaviest field of drifted snow that has fallen over the Midwest in memory. Indoors a battery of thermostats automatically control the desired temperature of each individual room. At hand are the amenities of modern life—good books, stereophonic music, radio, television, and a choice of fine food. Since my body from hours of indoor relaxation has temporarily been deprived of much nerve force and strength, a physically compelling desire obsesses me to remain within the warmth of my shelter—the list of attractive attributes and conveniences mentioned complementing this authority over the body.

On the other hand, knowing from planned experiment over many winters what departure from my present physical inactivity will bring, logic tells me that at the first opportunity, despite the indoor apathy toward a frigid atmosphere, I should venture outdoors to enjoy the durable benefits of a natural winter environment.

In a few hours, therefore, by calculated choice (I generally write in the morning), I will meet the outdoors on its own variable terms. Enjoying an unexplainable lust for the challenge of adverse weather—a sort of love for crisis all through life—I will venture outdoors on foot or on snowshoes with proper clothing no matter how rugged the weather, a blizzard, in truth, being preferred.

To all who have experienced this indoor-outdoor winter transition, the initial effect upon one's comfort will be apparent: For the first mile or so, the body suggests, though the mind tends to overrule, that a mistake has been made of even leaving the comfort of indoors at all.

Gradually, as travel proceeds, a change is sensed. The anatomical furnace, having been stoked with food before leaving, starts to generate natural heat—a physiological change from indoor torpor to outdoor animation that becomes surprisingly apparent. With every vigorous step one discovers that what seemed to be inadequate dress for the first mile now is becoming adequate, if not excessive. Garments require loosening. Instead of discomfort from the cold, a high state of physical and mental well-being is evident, a condition of cold that is felt to be not only tenable but highly desirable.

With an animated state of body and a new outlook, it is difficult to understand how one could possibly have held the sluggish indoor point of view about cold and snow that was coddled earlier. It is also equally difficult while bogged down with the lethargy of long, physically debilitating hours indoors to understand how one can have the invigorated state of mind and body one now possesses outdoors after the first mile or two of activity and climatic adjustment.

The premise here seems to be simple enough, but I think that we need to reflect most seriously on this important transitional factor, for it underlies our whole physical and mental reaction toward understanding the phenomena of winter and the very serious business of preserving life itself in its most vital state.

"Use it or lose it." This inescapable blessing or curse—however you wish to interpret the phrase—controls us all. The graph of our individual physical well-being is never static but continually either rising or falling. No physical condition remains so or improves without continual, deliberate physical effort. On the same premise, no mind remains spontaneously receptive and vigorous very long without constant intellectual cultivation and stimulation.

The skier, mountain climber, and others who pursue and enjoy winter activity will be aware of the physio-mental process just described. But what about that vast, captive urban population who daily cower from the cold? Transportation from home to office and return during a heavy snowfall or a sudden drop in temperature become for the majority an unpleasant encroachment on the "orderly" existence of modern industrial and business life.

Unfortunately, just about every aspect of urban existence is negative toward the advantages of winter. Superheated home, office, and factory require clothing adaptable to the indoors, with little immediate conversion-facility to cold and snow. Clothes fashions themselves, while they need not do so, play another role in raising the odds against the city dweller's adjustment to winter's advantages. With improper and inadequate clothing, the process of getting from home to work even in moderately inclement winter weather imposes varying degrees of discomfort, if not actual hardship, on the urban majority. And since the urban population lives in homes that are essentially machines, and their travel is primarily in machines, a snowstorm—natural and magnificent as it can be—instead of becoming an interesting phenomenon to enjoy, tends to foul up the mechanized order of their life, until season after season, city life, maladjusted to winter, sags into a kind of chronic discontent.

Man has largely been fighting the natural elements instead of adjusting to them since first he wandered away from nature's indispensable benefits. He has endeavored with tragic failure to substitute an increasingly artificial and consequently not a particularly happy life for his natural heritage. The city dweller, in his effort to make life viable in the zones of snow and cold, spends nearly his entire winter indoors under conditions seriously harmful to his respiratory system, which essentially means, by the complexity of advanced clinical standards, the continual lowering of his general health. He is not likely to exercise vigorously indoors, and if he does, under indoor winter conditions of extremely low humidity and unbalanced oxygenation, the exercise is of questionable benefit, if not harmful—at best a tragic and needless substitute for the refreshing outdoor life available to him by a few simple rules of daily application.

Once the urban population has been transported from home to work and return, infrequently does the pattern of physical inactivity change. Body, as we have seen, too generally controls mind—most often enslaves it. A five- to ten-mile winter walk daily after dinner is within the compass of most city dwellers and it can become highly desirable and enjoyable by the simple proposition described earlier in this chapter—mind over body the first mile or so. And once the city dweller has reached his home from office or plant, there should be nothing except major (not imagined) debility to prevent him from making an intelligent adjustment to a healthful, robust life. He may well recognize that after working hours, he need no longer be a cog in the city's machine, but a free agent, who by the mere act of choice must suffer serious physical degeneration in time unless he chooses to make a deliberate, natural, enjoyable adaption to his environment, regardless of season or inclemency of weather.

Earlier in life, when by imposed circumstance I was confined for a time to the city, I realized that it was not possible to walk vigorously an appreciable distance from home to job and arrive in a conventionally proper condition, despite the numerously propounded advantages of underarm anti-perspirants. But this posed no problem on the way home. I made a complete clothing adjustment to fit the elements before leaving the office and energetically walked the seven miles from office to home. After a shower and a change of clothes, I faced dinner with an appetite that required no pampering. The physically inactive evening that followed became alternatively a pleasant and beneficial diversion, rather than a harmful one, as a result of the exercise. No less did the following morning find me more eager for life and work by virtue of the previous evening's invigoration.

My wife and I now live in outer suburbia half of the year. The other half is spent in the wilderness. Some of our urban friends regard this mode of winter living in the country and wilderness as only adding to the "handicap of snow and cold." Yet, during the heavy winter already mentioned, and many others, we have moved but a few shovelfuls of snow, and we traveled about freely while most industrial, business, social, and domestic activity in the cities came to varying, periodical halts. The three hundred feet from our suburban dwelling to the highway is covered on snowshoes. When we are in the wilderness we depend entirely on snowshoes. After a number of snowshoe trips, the packed snow creates what is called a "snow bridge," on which one can walk without snowshoes. In suburbia when our car has no roads until plows open them, we sail along over the highest drifts at from twenty to twenty-five miles per hour in a motorized toboggan. The point is, we do not fight nature, we accept it on friendly terms and deeply enjoy its variable moods. While we applied variations of procedure to meet a different set of circumstances, our earlier years within the city were no more at odds with winter.

Since man, in order to survive even moderate temperatures, must resort to the artificial covering of his body, it may be assumed that primordially he may have been a tropical animal. Yet, if we are to judge the comparative progress he has made in warm areas of the world with those of the cold, he seems to accomplish most in colder climates. Strangely, this has applied as well to his mental efforts as to his physical accomplishments. We have seen how any intellectually creative work drops markedly in the heat of summer and rises measurably in the cold of winter.

I might even boldly suggest that if the history of civilization shows an appreciable intellectual advantage in the colder latitudes, is not man a superior creature as he adjusts to the cold?

A great deal of misinformation existed in early days about the white man's failure to live in the Far North—the only adaptable race capable of doing so, it was believed, being the Eskimo. Down through years of arctic exploration it has been found that living in the cold regions is no more difficult physically for one race than another, regardless of color, although something might perhaps be said for the distinction between Eskimo and white racial temperaments. In the final analysis, adjustment to cold, we have learned, becomes largely a matter of metabolism. Tests of a preponderantly meat diet in winter have proved this to be the race-equalizing factor in adjusting to cold temperatures. For example, Peary in his trek to the North Pole said that the best arctic traveling companion he had was Matt Henson, an American Negro.

Man, as indicated earlier, has managed with his increasing affluence and mechanical mobility to carry on a massive north-south seasonal migration. The primary purpose of the southward movement has been, of course, to flee from the cold and snow. The southerner moves north in summer to avoid the heat, but with the advent of air conditioning, many southerners have been content to remain in their high-temperature zones. Tragically, both appear willing to suffer what might seem like penal confinement within the walls of home, office, and factory, if a "comfortable" temperature, even though poorly humidified, can artificially be maintained. Thus, man's resignation to an indoor, lethargic existence in both the north and the south is becoming seriously damaging to our national general health.

Willful thinking too readily lends itself to argument against a physically active life. Creativity and the fruits of genius, we are often led to believe, come from a sedentary existence. It has been suggested that when an individual feels a great satisfaction in the overpowering vitality of excellent health and high spirit, he is more content to live with physical pleasures than to engage in intellectual effort. Willful thinking and the insidious plea for a sedentary life thus argue forcefully to avoid physical activity, with consequent poor health and on the whole a questionable happiness.

I do not go along with the view that sedentary life makes for intellectual stimulation, nor do the facts bear out this theory. A sedentary life might be a factor in favor of grinding out paper work; as Sinclair Lewis said in essence, successful writing is the ability to "apply the seat of the pants to the seat of the chair." On the other hand, a three-hour snowshoe trek across the hills, or a vigorous walk in the city, prepares the mind more assiduously to "apply the seat of the pants to the seat of the chair." One reads and writes with regained pleasure and, I am sure, with a more vital reaction to the subject matter. The same applies to enjoyment of stereophonic music before an open fire. I find that when the body has been relaxed by exercise the mind becomes a great deal more receptive to the finer nuances and values of composition. When I read with pent-up physical energy, my mind strays from the printed page into a thought vacuum, until I merely scan what I read without truly enjoying or assimilating the author's point of view. I have been told by the sedentary set that when one feels an overwhelming desire to exercise, all one need do is to lie down for a while and the desire will go away. The road to enervation, we may be sure, is that smoothly paved. Comfort comes into one's home, remains, and in time becomes a master. I believe it was Hemingway who said that "fattening of the body can lead to fattening of the mind." Perhaps he might also have added that succumbing wholly to enervating comfort is gradually to surrender, much too early, life itself.

2

ESCAPE COMPLEX

How does one go about proving that life below zero can be not only healthful but viable, animated, enjoyable, and inestimably fruitful? The most vital and convincing proof I know of took place in the wilderness of upper Lake Winnipeg in Manitoba, Canada, a good many years ago. If I may be allowed to use a single example here through an entire chapter, perhaps the reader will find it significant, possibly interesting, even, I hope, convincing.

A middle-aged, former Chicago businessman and his nineteen-year-old daughter, on a late fall boat excursion on Lake Winnipeg, followed by a two-weeks' stay in a cabin, had missed the last boat back for the city of Winnipeg.

Panic seized the pair. The possibility of getting caught in the freeze-up of Lake Winnipeg's shore ice excluded the trip south by canoe and paddle. It was the era before radio communication or planes. Also, the outboard motor idea at that time was just beginning to germinate in the head of Ole Evinrude, its inventor.

I was laying over in the summer cabin of a trapper friend at the upper end of the lake, waiting for the freeze-up swing-over from canoe to dog sled travel. The only existing, immediate alternative in view for the father and daughter was to wait for the freeze-up and travel south with me by dog sled. The father was a bit paunchy, the daughter young and attractive, but with only a little more athletic prowess to travel three hundred miles on snowshoes than the father. The travel outlook for both was a bit grim. My harness dogs were calculated to haul a sled loaded with light, portable, winter camp equipment, provisions, and dog feed—not passengers. Would I have a potential coronary on my hands somewhere along this three-hundred-mile wild shore, with little chance of hauling a two-hundred-pound man or a girl, or both? The Indians who might possibly have been hired to haul the pair in dog sled carrioles had departed to interior trap lines for the winter.

My time of departure south by dog sled was contingent upon the degree of temperature drop, varying in uncertainty from week to week. With his industrial influence and apparent affluence, the father of the stranded pair, I presumed, was more accustomed to giving orders than taking them. Nevertheless, I made it realistically clear that if we were to travel together on this trip, it would be necessary that he diet and seek some conditioning in the meantime. The reducing diet seemed no problem at the time, since he could do it chiefly on a protein diet of meat. My own diet—as at the beginning of every winter—had for a month been primarily meat for the purpose of raising my metabolism to cope with cold weather. Moose, woodland caribou, and bear meat here at this wilderness camp at that time were far more plentiful than conventional store trade foods.

With some affairs of my own to attend to inland from Lake Winnipeg toward Hudson Bay, I did not see the stranded tourists during the ensuing two weeks. They had, however, been well accommodated in a log cabin. Both father and daughter, I learned, had made a desperate effort during my absence to abide by the rather strict rules of exercise and diet I had laid down. They were seriously convinced that "escape to the outside" depended on these instructions. And so, perhaps, it did. But it occurred to me that, above all, a wintering in this Northern region might have been what both of them needed physically and mentally, more than "escape" to the city.

Lake Winnipeg's waters were now churning roughly, which they especially do in late fall, to escape, it seemed, the bonds of winter that would soon be encroaching upon their wash of these wilderness shores. The temperature was moving consistently downward. The last days of my inland trip had been threatened by thin ice that had to be broken by riding up on the surface and breaking it down with an improvised icebreaker made from a wooden crotch fastened to the canoe bow. Lake Winnipeg's shore also was becoming ice-encrusted as the last breakers sent a freezing spray flying well up onto the land, creating fantastic crystalline shapes on rocks and shore brush.

My dogs seemed to sense by the increasing cold that soon they would be on the move, if I can presume that they remembered their few seasonal changes. Even during off-feed times, whenever I approached them they became wild with excitement for the trail. As I gave each a caressing rub around the ears, I assured them, "It won't be long now."

These dogs had been reared and trained with a kindly hand and no whip. While I showed them occasional affection out of harness, once they were in harness they were never touched except for unharnessing or to stop an occasional fight. This is not so much a matter of personal attitude as one of good harness-dog training policy. My stranded tourists visited the dogs but were asked not to make pets of them. With a one-quarter wolf strain, the demeanor of these dogs and their size did not exactly invite the extended, caressing hand of strangers.

One morning I discovered a calm lake and ice tentacles reaching out into the water some little distance. But before the day was well under way a wind came up, crumbling the ice, sending plate glass-like sheets slithering onto the shore. This alternate freeze and breakup was repeated several times. Finally, a morning did come when calm and cold persisted throughout the day and into the night. The ice held. The brooding, contrasting silence that ensued left no doubt as to what was happening. This adjustment of mind and inner ear from the constant roar of breaking waves pounding a rough coast to a suddenly imposed winter silence leaves a strange, peaceful mood on some people; on others a disturbing, ominous dread. The time of open water travel in the North was over for another season.

To skirt the icebound shore of Lake Winnipeg by dog sled in winter, or by canoe during open water, requires the crossing of many bays. One must keep travel out beyond the headlands in order to shorten the route. While ice was forming quite fast in the bays, it formed less rapidly around headland water. It was apparent that considerable time was yet needed for the subzero nights to get in their work before our shore travel could safely proceed. My trail companions-to-be were growing both apprehensive and restless. Now and then, they seemed to be suppressing a feeling of desperation. Not fully comprehending what was in store for them, they felt both a desire to stay in the safety of a warm cabin and a need to get on the trail toward home.

From the interior Indians I had acquired woven rabbit-skin (snowshoe hare) sleeping robes, moosehide moccasins, mittens and snowshoes. While making these purchases, I was told by the Indians that they did not consider it feasible to abandon their trap lines to haul the stranded tourists out by dog carriole, nor by the Indians' own standards did they consider the

tourists' plight an emergency, or, for that matter, even significant.

Rabbit-skin robes are exceptionally warm and excellent for
winter travel, but shed badly. For this reason, it was necessary
to quilt the robes with a light cotton fabric covering obtained
from a small inland Post. The hand-sewing job was turned
over to the future users and not only kept them busy but gave
them an intimate insight into the material actualities of trail
equipment. Quilting, I found, greatly increases the warmth of
these rabbit-skin robes.

Caribou-fur parkas; moosehide, smoke-tanned Indian moccasins; wool socks; duffel socks; calf moosehide mittens lined
with duffel, the mittens dangling from moosehide thongs—
these items in themselves when tried out around the cabin area
had the properties of building up the morale of my trail mates
and offering them a heretofore unknown sense of security from
the elements. Natives had custom-made the parkas.

Duffel is a heavy, high-grade wool material that is a little
denser than blanketing and somewhat looser than wool felt. It
is used for low socks, mitten and parka linings, as well as
parkas themselves. Duffel is sold by the yard and can be pro-
cured at Hudson's Bay Posts.

Since the father had offered to pay generously for any items
he and his daughter would need, I saw to it that the Indians
were more than well paid for the clothing items, and so they
gladly supplied their best. But when it came to the wool
underwear purchased at the Post, the morale barometer
dropped suddenly. Neither of my stranded tourists believed
they could tolerate the itchy effect.

Although I assured them that the itch would leave very soon
on the trail, my companions' look of skepticism nearly wilted
my own long-established confidence in the garments. The mistake of donning woolly long johns in a heated cabin, probably
at a temperature of 80 or better, was, of course, the real problem. They itched, sweated, and flushed, while I explained that
the garments would best be laundered before we could start in

order to remove perspiration salt residue, and that when they actually dressed for the trail, it would have to be done in a cool to cold room. Perspiration from accumulating residual salts in undergarments and sleeping bags has traditionally been the insidious enemy stalking the winter trail.

If problem one was itchy underwear, problem two moved in when they learned that their Gladstone bags and other luggage, with nearly all of the contents, would have to be left behind to follow seven months later on the first spring boat. The thought of arriving in Winnipeg with no other garments than the backwoods garb they would wear on the trail, plus a spare suit of woolen underwear and some heavy wool socks, seemed to them both embarrassing and amusing. The feminine member of our party, however, rather enjoyed the novel prospect of a full-scale shopping spree in Winnipeg, dressed, as she would be, in an Indian-made caribou parka and moccasins.

"This should be interesting," she commented, "if we ever get to Winnipeg."

Fear of the unknown is understandable. Since I had regarded winter travel by dog sled no more hazardous than any other form of transportation, to me getting to Winnipeg was simply winter camp and travel routine. I now experience more apprehension on a thousand-mile, commercial jet plane, instrument flight through a blinding snowstorm over the mountains than I ever have while traveling by dog sled, guided by compass and the general nature of the terrain, through even a wilderness blizzard.

All seems to depend on our environmental training. A few years ago while on a canoe voyage through the white-water-strewn Berens River in Manitoba, I came upon two Indians who had been freighting supplies to Little Grand Rapids Post. One expressed a lurid curiosity about the city of Winnipeg and its "hazards." Finally he said, "If I can ever pick up enough guts, I am going there sometime." This from a man who spent season after season shooting dangerous rapids in a canoe on a dozen or more Canadian rivers, and driving dogs over as many questionable river-ice trails.

Knowing that increasing apprehensions did exist with the father and daughter, and to avoid their tossing in bed through the night and coming up unrested, I did not prepare them the night before for the morning takeoff.

From the low reading of my field thermometer I could tell that for some time ice was forming exceptionally fast— freezing speeded up by a lack of snow covering. (Ice increases its thickness rapidly when thin, slower in direct ratio to its thickness.) The last day before our departure the temperature rose to a thaw, a cloud cover came over, and an inch or less of snow became well bonded to the ice by the higher temperature. By morning the temperature again dropped well below zero. This frozen, previously thawed snow-cover offered a crusty, secure footing and fast sledding.

I packed camp equipment, provisions, and dog feed on the sled the night before in a cold cache shed to keep it safe from the depredations of any loose, prowling dogs or forest creatures, especially the possible visit of a wolverine.

The sled used was the basket or carriole type, with upstands or handlebars, made sturdier than the lighter racing unit in order to carry the standard camp equipment load required on the trail.

For days previous to the start, I had been making large batches of stewed meat with brown gravy in an oven. The finished product in a large, flat, square pan was set out in sub-zero weather. As the stew began to slush-freeze, a knife was drawn down through it and across until rectangular portions of meal-ration size for three people began to freeze and hold to the division lines. As freezing progressed, the knife was redrawn again and again along the division lines until the stew was frozen brick-hard; the pan was then heated just enough to allow the entire mass to drop loose in one piece from the pan onto the bottom of a box. There with sharp blows from a camp ax the stew was broken along the knife fissures into meal-size bricks and wrapped in waxed paper for the trail. The waxed paper used was heavy Manila wrapping paper, which I had painted with hot paraffin.

A large quantity of doughnuts had also been made and packed for "mug-ups"—the coffee breaks along the trail.

Doughnut dunking probably had its origin on the winter trail. Mine I always prethaw in camp the night before, wrapping and placing them with the thermos coffee bottle in a well-insulated bag. The mug-up is thus expedited and with no dunking of frozen doughnuts, the coffee stays hot longer in the cup.

Quantities of the stewed meat in bricks individually wrapped; slabs of rich, individually wrapped fruitcake; doughnuts, rice, coffee, tea, cocoa, dried apples and apricots; a mix of flour, baking powder, dried milk, sugar, salt, and shortening for bannock; and dried whole milk comprised the simple but adequate fare for the trip. Some Swedish rye crisp and a few dozen pilot biscuits were added the last minute for convenience in the early camps.

Note that the list contains a rather unusual item for the wilderness—fruitcake. This is a compact, high-caloric food. When properly made with nuts, raisins, currants, citron, sugar, eggs, milk, fruit juices, butter, etc., it is a balanced meal in itself. I used a great deal of it, and on those arctic expeditions over subsequent years where I planned the equipment and food budget for others, fruitcake proved to be a valuable addition, giving a certain gastronomic excitement to the short noonday stop for lunch. It became, as it were, a sort of luxurious K ration.

The cold weather tent used—a modified wedge type made of sailcloth—is so constructed as to accommodate a second, inner tent, spaced about two inches or less from the outside unit and held in place with tie tapes. This creates a dead-air space between the two units, providing valuable insulation.

The tent heating unit is a small-size, light, sheet metal stove, commonly known as an "airtight." It is vented with a four-inch pipe through a thimble, set between the flaps of the tent opening. A backdraft is installed in the pipe to control a slow, all-night fire. Short-length stovepipe sections are used so they can be stored in the stove for convenient transportation between camps.

It was this kind of equipment and the adventurous prospect it held forth that greeted my stranded trail companions as I hustled them out of bed, sleepy-eyed and apprehensive, two hours before daylight on a not too cold, clear, star-studded morning. Days are short and nights long in the Northern winter. Breakfast was eaten leisurely with many cups of coffee, while I laid down a brief for the day's activities ahead, even explaining how they might go about most comfortably performing their urgent body functions in sub-zero temperatures and snow that could be waist-deep. A square of turned-up birch bark is used as a receptacle, the function performed in it inside the warm tent, and immediate disposition made in the wood stove. The bark creates a quick hot flame, and with ventilation no factor in a tent, all is *sans gêne*.

The dogs, frantic to get going, were not easily held back the first few miles, but finally they settled down to that pace which is neither walking nor running for man—a killing gait until one gets used to it, if in truth this can ever be fully accomplished. For this reason I had my trail companions start out along the shore well ahead of me so that I could set a fast enough pace to take the edge off the dogs' wild exuberance. By the time I and the dogs caught up, it was time for the first mug-up.

The big secret of winter travel, as I have indicated, is to start with maximum clothing and keep shedding the outer items long before very much body-generated heat is felt. My companions took this advice very seriously and quickly grasped the principle. When I reached them, I was pleased to see that they were carrying their parkas, their duffel-lined moosehide mit-

"The initial day of travel had been concluded."

tens dangling at the cord ends, hands bare at a temperature around zero.

The first move when gaining natural animal heat is to loosen the assumption sash—a moosehide ribbon, or sometimes a colorful wool-braided band or sash that is tied around the waist of the parka. Some parkas have a built-in drawstring for this purpose. Removing the sash lets cool air under the parka. Next, the parka is opened at the throat and the hood is thrown back, the head covering now being only a stocking cap or ski cap. Finally, the parka is removed entirely. There are times, of course, during extreme travel conditions when the parka cannot be removed, but in any event, one constantly holds fast to the principle of being underdressed rather than overdressed as physical activity begins to warm the body.

After the mug-up our party swung on down the lake past the noon stop, but being lean and hard myself, I kept on going until my companions started showing signs of a slight, stumbling weariness. I then turned the dogs—a little soft from inactivity—into an opening in the coniferous forest, staked them out in a protected area, and built a large, open campfire. Soon I had the tent up and a fire going in the airtight within. The initial day of travel had been concluded. I was well pleased with the results.

The tent soon warmed up as a fire crackled comfortably in the airtight. A bed of spruce and balsam boughs allowed the sleeping robes to be rolled out. My trail companions stretched out, amazed that such comfort could be established in the wilderness in so short a time and with what, condensed in the shoulder packsacks, seemed to be such meager facilities. After a short rest, though with some stiffness, they were soon boiling rice and warming stewed meat on the stove. An aluminum pail, repeatedly filled with snow, had been set on the back of the stove for tea and for water in which to boil the rice. This melting of snow had to be done in such a manner that the snow did not blot up the water, leaving the inside bottom of the pail dry to score from the heat. Some terribly foul-tasting tea brews and food have been the result of such scoring. When melting snow, it must continually be forced to the bottom of the pail until a liberal pool of water forms. (Lake Winnipeg has mud-silted water that needs filtering, so I preferred to use water from snow. Later in the winter the ice in this lake loses the silt near the surface by a gravitational leaching and can then be melted for beverage water.)

"A weasel . . . dodged in and out of the down timber"

Food for the dogs I cooked on the outside open fire, the flames lending truth as they always do to Sabin's famous, delightful lines:

> "Cold night weighs down the forest bough,
>   Strange shapes go flitting through the gloom,
>   But see, a spark, a flame, the wilderness is home."

A weasel, now in his white winter coat and black-tipped tail, dodged in and out of the down timber, sniffing the air to get on the aromatic beam of the fish and cereal that was being cooked for the dogs. I cut a piece of raw fish and tied it to a cord, dangling it from a low limb. Once the weasel bit into it, he swung clear of his footing and performed a dozen highly amusing aerial acrobatic stunts in the process of eating and trying to carry off the fish.

Absolute calm hung over the winter forest. The occasional crackle of the fire and our subdued voices were the only intrusions upon the utter winter silence. Earlier the loud whacks of my ax and the hiss of my saw sounded natural enough in a man's world, but as evening crept in, any noise would have seemed a desecration. The dogs rested, always with a cocked and confident eye for the feed they knew would soon be served them—ravenously to bolt it down in a matter of seconds, then sniff around for a salient, overlooked crumb.

An influence strange and grand had affected my companions. Hunched up in their caribou parkas on a log before an open fire they watched the dog feed cooking and contemplated the surrounding forest with an apparent mixture of mystery, weariness, and a growing satisfaction from achievement. A note of theatrical gaiety had been contributed by the weasel's comic performance, while a stock repertoire of trail stories lent a further casualness to what might otherwise have seemed an adventure to them—a frame of mind I wanted to avoid until they were more adjusted to their trail environment.

Now in their minds at least was the certainty of a warm bed—something on which they had speculated with deep concern back in their rented cabin on the north end of the lake. Their physical needs having been taken care of with substantial trail food, a deep introspection seemed to dominate their thoughts as to what actually was happening to them in this strange wilderness.

From their places on the log before the fire, they rose quite stiffly and crawled into rabbit-skin robes for the night. If concern had dogged their minds during the last few weeks at the upper end of Lake Winnipeg, the way they slept was proof that much of their apprehension had flown. They did take a pain-killer at bedtime, I learned, to quiet the ache of muscular fatigue. Once during the night the wild howl of a timber wolf aroused the dogs and set up their wolfish howling in accompaniment, which awakened all of us. But as our lady remarked, "Even though I felt a bit frightened, I wouldn't have missed that wild howl in the wilderness night for the world!"

The stove poked slowly along throughout the sleeping hours, controlled by the backdraft, with just enough heat barely to cut the frosty edge of night. All of us slept snug and warm in

". . . the wild howl of a timber wolf . . ."

our rabbit-skin robes. Eight hours later, I closed the backdraft in the stove, refilled the stove with wood, and opened the main draft. A rhythmic roar soon made a red-hot spot on the top surface, which was conveniently and duly capped with the coffee pail. Coffee aroma must have roused more people from their early-morning beds throughout the world than any other inducer of activity ever discovered by man.

No eggs, toast, or orange juice were on our breakfast menu, but the three of us did well on stewed moose meat, hot bannock, coffee, and stewed apricots. We fed a pair of Whiskey

"... we noisily swung out ... onto Lake Winnipeg ... and headed
south again."

Jacks (Canada Jays) that showed up at daylight, hung another
piece of raw fish on the "trapeze" string for the weasel, and
with the dogs setting up a great hullabaloo to get going, we
noisily swung out of the deep, coniferous forest onto Lake
Winnipeg's expansive three hundred miles of ice, and headed
south again.

The weather held a delightful calm day after day, mostly
just a few degrees below zero, occasionally above, sometimes
at night down to 15 below, until we reached the mouth of the
Poplar River. We had been getting a good suntan. Also, I was

pleased to find that my companions, though quite stiff in the morning, managed to work it off the first hour or so on the trail, and were able to travel a little farther each day. (We can afford to be lean and hard.)

By now my trail mates had learned something of dog sled travel and winter camping, which made my own routine camp chores lighter. Clothes were beginning to take on the used impress of their wearers, assimilated to each individual's character. But the best part was that daily my companions were showing a need for fewer clothes. Much of the time the parkas were riding under the lash ropes of the sled, being donned only at mug-up stops and around camp. Their city pallor had given way to the flush of stronger circulation and apple-red cheeks.

The dogs were daily getting into better physical condition, losing some of their accumulated summer fat. (They too need to be kept lean and hard.) At times they paused and rolled in the snow to cool off, even though the temperature was well below zero. "When you feel like that in midwinter," the father commented, "I would say you have it made."

At the Poplar River camp we began striking higher temperatures and snow—lots of it. A heavy wind was driving the falling snow horizontally shoreward from the northwest. Visibility became poor, and it seemed wise to get a good rest during the storm. From now on it was apparent that much of the trip would have to be on snowshoes—something we had managed to avoid up to this time on the snow-crusted ice. My trail companions had never used snowshoes, and viewed them with questionable confidence. In the howling gale, alternately on drifted snow and exposed, windblown spots of ice, I gave snowshoe lessons, warning of the danger that inflammation of the leg tendons (*mal de racquette*) might entail.

The snowstorm raged on all day with seemingly relentless fury, but broke sometime after midnight. By the following morning the temperature had dropped so low—to minus 48—it still seemed unwise to travel. A sort of brooding silence reigned over a magnificent landscape. The predominantly spruce and balsam forest rising from our camp seemed to impart an ominous stillness in the deep snow and cold, except for the occasional gunshot-like report from the expanding trees. The vent pipe from our tent sent smoke straight up, scarcely wavering, until it was dissipated in the thinner upper atmosphere. Cold at almost 50 below entailed a three-day layover, which after the first day began to worry my companions. I sensed a deep, moody terror in any reference to the temperature.

On the fourth day a rather freakish and fortunate change took place. The wind rose rapidly from the south, the temperature rising to 10 below before noon. We broke camp. Travel became a delight. Spirits rose with every proportionate rise of temperature. Slight frostbite had been suffered by the father, who had earlier thrown back the hood of his parka too long when the temperature was almost a minus 50. This, however, caused very little eventual difficulty, and it had the value of being an early warning against carelessness.

Travel was slowed down, of course, by the snow and the beginner snowshoers. Camps were pitched with many less miles accomplished each day. Learning to travel on snowshoes some casual afternoon for pleasant recreation in a rural countryside is quite different from day-after-day travel in the wilderness to reach a distant objective. At the upper end of the lake before the journey started, there was an apparent deep concern which left my companions once travel got well under way. Now, as they found travel slowed down with snowshoes, their spirits again began to sag. Wearily they slogged along. My banter to keep up their spirits got only mild, polite response.

At the end of each day, to ward off possible *mal de racquette*, I had them soak the lower part of their legs in hot water, heated in the large pail used for cooking dog feed. It was now necessary for me to break trail ahead of the dogs, as we encountered innumerable high, knife-edged drifts around the headlands. The trailbreaking allowed my companions somewhat better going on their not too well behaved snowshoes. Several days later they had accomplished much with their snowshoeing, and were able to spell me off for short periods on the trailbreaking. They seemed to have become quite adept on the rapidly packed snow of the lake, even when mounting average drifts. But confidence in their growing experience paled as we turned inland to a camp area. In the deep, soft, unpacked snow of the heavy forest over down timber, sharp turns, and rough terrain, they floundered at times, I thought, a little pathetically. Nevertheless, their difficulties were met with outward good humor and a realization that snowshoeing like most everything else needs more than a first, impetuous effort. Camp followed camp, varied somewhat by changing moods of weather and the occasional sight of wildlife; travel became largely routine. Conversation had now dwindled to bare essentials only. Humans and dogs had fallen into a set of trail reflexes where it seemed no special instructions any longer need be applied to the daily routine.

The last camp of the journey was pitched along the bank of the Red River. The temperature hovered only a little below zero. I thought it would be an occasion for joy and celebration on the part of my trail mates. Somehow, however, a secondary gloom had come over them. Both had reached a point now, with three hundred miles of foot and snowshoe travel behind them, where their bodies had sloughed off the debilitating fat and lethargy of urban life. They had experienced and were enjoying an invigoration and a body tone unknown to them in their adult lives, being able to travel from daylight until dark, with only the degree of fatigue that makes the night's rest exquisite. Earlier in the journey, they had taken spoonfuls of pain-killer nightly to relieve the muscular ache in their legs. Now the pain-killer no longer was needed.

Here was a father forty-two years of age and a daughter nineteen, winding up an experience of great personal significance to them. I believed, because of their early apprehensions, that getting to the outside world had been their innermost desire. My job was nearly accomplished, and I was about to receive payment accordingly. Outside of that, the undiminished lust for wilderness travel, and the amicable companionship I enjoyed, the process of getting them to the railhead for their return to Chicago seemed rather a normal procedure. It had in the broadest sense been no particular adventure for me but rather another wilderness-rewarding journey and, in those low-budget days, a chance to earn some money. My dogs, now content to rest, were boarded out on the Red River bank with a friend, my trail guests and I making the remaining miles into the city of Winnipeg with a hired team of horses, bobsled, and driver. Bundled up in our rabbit-skin sleeping robes deep in hay at the bottom of the wagon box, I was, I admit, enjoying the brief diversion of no longer being the "driver."

As we dined lavishly in Winnipeg's finest hotel, my companions' sadness increased. At my then youthful age, I did not fully grasp the significance of what they revealed over the meal—but I do now. This, they said, was the first truly great experience of their lives, and would probably be their last "wilderness adventure." They had lived most of their lives up to then by the dictates of urban circumstance—a life of conventionality with affluence. It was a life with little physical activity, and it would no doubt now be circumstantially continued. When they missed the last boat at the upper end of the lake, the most fortunate play of events, they explained, had befallen them. Only by being stranded would they ever have had the courage, they said, to set out on such a dog sled journey. They confessed to having entertained a mortal fear of dying on the trail from exposure or a possible crippling coronary. But their apprehension had vanished as we made camp after camp, until they had developed a rich and abiding confidence in the wilderness and in themselves.

From weeks of travel through Canada's winter wilderness, they had reached that ascendancy of physical well-being known only to few. Now they were at a point when their bodies and minds were attuned to nature. They had come to recognize its vibrant effect in the most self-evident sense. Life would soon inadvertently have to sink back into a conventional if not languid conformity, and having peeked momentarily into paradise below zero, their mundane lives could never again be quite the same.

3

THE
WHITE WILDERNESS

WE might conclude in contrast with the foregoing that the white wilderness as featured in derring-do fiction has created a generally false, if not frightening, impression by comparison— more confusing and deceiving than educating. Personally, however, I have found that these fictitious tales have not been entirely without romantic merit. In my youth as I read the fancied stories of how the wolf pack attacked the wilderness traveler, how rows of green eyes glowed and glared outside his night campfire—the wolves fearing only the flaming fagots thrown at them to keep them at bay—I became irresistibly engrossed in wilderness adventure.

The deceptions will probably never fully catch up with their authors; thus the charm of the deceptive fiction eternally lingers. If only these tales were true—what an adventure such wilderness life could be! I can see the overturned sled used as a barricade in a howling blizzard, wolves—fangs bared—

closing in, while the Winchester carbine barks out in staccato blasts to stem the encroaching pack.

But alas, this kind of adventure was not to be. Wolves, unfortunately, do not comply with the pseudo-adventure of fictional fancy. They attack human beings only in print or TV skits. In fact, the mere scent of a man sends timber wolves on a wide, circumspective detour. No wolfish eyes, I soon sadly discovered, glow and glare in the night at the fringe of winter wilderness campfires. One could tramp from Cape Horn to the arctic archipelago without the need of a firearm as protection from a premeditated attack by wilderness creatures.

Recently, I read a story about the weasel, what a cunning and vicious creature it is. The weasel, the author claimed, will waylay and leap into the face of a forest traveler, in an effort to attach itself to the jugular vein of a man's throat. A weasel that can find its way into a cabin through some opening, he continued, is sure to reach a sleeper and suck his blood. And so the fictional fraud goes on. At both wilderness cabin and camp, on many occasions, I have managed to bait-in one of these fascinating creatures with pieces of raw fish, just for the joy of its friendliness and the fun of seeing it perform its various capers. A red squirrel, contrary to general opinion, will send a weasel scurrying in high retreat, and I have wondered what the end result would be in an actual confrontation. I would be inclined to bet on the red squirrel. The weasel is a harmless, valuable pet to have around a cabin for keeping down mice, although it does not seem to adapt very well to prolonged domestic habitat. It loves too well the free run of wild stream and lakeshore.

Does this imply that adventure is no part of the white wilderness? Indeed not, but if mortal combat with forest creatures is the substance of such adventure, the answer is yes. On the other hand, the winter wilderness is enough of a challenge and adventure without the fearsome illusion of "fighting off wild beasts."

"I would be inclined to bet on the red squirrel."

We can afford to be honest, I think, in our depiction of the wilderness. It can prove no less interesting. Hunters, who never stir from their metropolitan homes unless to kill something afield that dearly wanted to live, who are addicted to slaughter, try desperately, of course, to show a fierce opponent in their prey and a virility in themselves to justify the act of destroying some hapless wild creature for pleasure.

"The dreadful, bitter cold," "the savage wilderness"—these were some of the threats handed down to me as I first entered the wilderness. "The wilderness must be conquered," "An undeveloped wilderness is a sinful waste" are the periodic utterances of ecological immaturity.

Conquer a friend? The preservation of natural beauty a sin? Asphalt the more desirable trail to happiness?

To unlearn in adulthood what in such large measure we are speciously taught in youth—must this always be the process of much education?

On the strength of this pseudo-knowledge, I approached the wilderness in my youth with a suspicion of bitterness, savagery, and sinfulness. I was on guard, prepared for every hostile eventuality. I found in nature instead a cooperative friendship, abundance, generosity, and certainly amorality. With these attributes I have lived close to the natural world well over a half century—finding it increasingly enchanting, infinitely complex in interest, priceless in value, durable in benefit beyond the profoundest understanding and broadest appraisal. As Wordsworth said, "Nature never did betray the heart that loved her."

In about two hours, this writing, which is now being continued in my wilderness cabin in Ontario, Canada, will be laid aside for the remainder of the day. In a setting of last night's unbroken, newly fallen snow, I will reopen the ice fishing hole and likely catch a lake trout for supper. One fish and that will be it, for I am not inclined to the practice of viewing outdoor life primarily in terms of fish and game pounds. And there is a pretty good chance that because I do not derive pleasure from the misery of a fish struggling for its life at the end of the line, I will not exhaust the catch there, but will manage a fish from the hole only when I wish to satisfy this particular caprice of appetite.

Yesterday, I snowshoed to Lake Getchigami via the North River. Wild animal tracks—some fresh, some old—crisscrossed and ran parallel with the river. Last night's snowfall obliterated all tracks, as though nature were erasing her board for a new lesson in natural history. Most likely, I will see fresh

"*I . . . established salt licks for the moose to draw them into focus . . .*"

moose tracks where the browse is thickest, and perhaps see the animals themselves in a secluded yard, if I follow a fresh trail long enough. Moose create these yards when the snow becomes very deep by heavily tramping down the snow in an area. Here they find protection from the wind; they can congregate, loiter, and lie down. I have baited-in a few places for sight of the carnivores and established salt licks for the moose to draw them into the focus of my camera.

One of these carnivore baiting places is at a small open area of water near a falls. Last week an otter caught and killed a fish there. The crimson snow, fish scales, and otter tracks were obvious signs to read. If I am lucky today, the otter will be back to get my bait. That is, he will try to carry it off, but I

An otter on the ice near open water after having caught and killed a fish

have so secured it that only by perseverance can he get a small portion at a time. In this fashion he will be kept there until I can manage the desired telephoto photography.

What exquisite beauty can possibly rival that of newly fallen snow? Each evergreen spruce and balsam frond holds a scintillating white pillow. Sunlight on the lake's snowfield imparts a dazzling purity as though all the desecrations of man had suddenly vanished. Too bad in some ways, that the new snowfall cannot remain undisturbed. This afternoon I will disturb it, though reluctantly, as I again break a trail across the lake and up the river. Tomorrow morning when I look out over the lake, the sensuous curves of my snowshoe tracks will be there, delineating and revealing every meandering move I make—providing, of course, that the wind does not drift them over. Even then, a trained woodsman could follow the trail and reveal much of my activity.

". . . strange shapes and shadows form here and there . . ."

Most of us are appalled by the silence of a white, sub-zero wilderness. Where the muffled steps of snowshoes are the only audible sound, the overwhelming silence in a world of white is bound to be profoundly mystifying. Now and then, the cold will expand a tree with a loud echoing report, but the ensuing silence seems deepened by it. Stop to listen and all stands silent—to some, a brooding, despairing silence; to all, a mysterious silence. In the growing season the forest undergoes conspicuous change. Now all, except animal life, is held in frigid suspension. It is strange when you think of it—that in this season of static cold, no vegetation grows, nor does anything decay—almost a frightening suspension, as though the world had stopped its metamorphic progression.

At this season in the North the sun cuts a low declination arc over the sky, scarcely rising above the forest before it sets. Day is all too short. Consequently, I will be returning to my cabin

". . . an owl swoops from river bank to river bank . . ."

under cover of darkness. Toward dusk, strange shapes and
shadows form here and there—most are as immobile as the
winter night, but some truly move. Snowshoe hares, white as
the snow, scamper spookily about; an owl or two swoops from
river bank to river bank on silent, phantomlike wings, while
some imagined, some real creatures lurk in the shadows.

I am aware that forest creatures are watching me from their
seclusion. I have been seen by fox and timber wolf from time
to time, because their unmistakable tracks have appeared during the interval of my passing through. If wolves show up
actually to be seen at times, which is extremely rare, it is only
that they want to steal a fleeting, distant glimpse, prompted by
curiosity. Most often they dare not risk even this momentary
indulgent look.

Since activity tends to keep me in good physical condition at
all times, I will not be especially weary when I reach the

cabin. Nevertheless, a pot of coffee, an open fire, and a rest
with a good book will prove pleasantly diversionary. It being
the month of February, I am apt to give pause in my reading
—for off in the hills will likely come the most arresting winter
call of the Northland—the howl of a timber wolf. I will don
my parka and silently slip out into the winter night. When the
howl comes again, this time not muffled by my cabin walls or
accompanied by the crackling sound of my fire and the tick of
my clock, it will be like a beseeching call out of eternity—
lonely, mournful, almost despairing. Some people have told
me that their flesh creeps when they hear the howl of a timber
wolf. Personally, I experience an overwhelming sympathy—a
desire to walk out there in the black void of night and rub the
ears of this magnificent creature, if I could, as I might a sled
dog whose kinship by inbreeding has become traditionally a
part of that howl.

Some of us who live a part of life in the white wilderness of
the North are torn between the attraction of the forest and the
inexplicable lure of the open arctic Barrens. One is at a loss to
know how a land seemingly as barren as the arctic prairie can
draw interest with such magnetic force. For a number of years
I considered that my wilderness interest would always end at
the northern tree lines. In this same sense I had looked upon
the Southwest desert. The Southwest mountains, yes, but never
the desert, I broadly asserted. In time, as the saying goes, I
came to eat crow—feathers and all.

The more I ponder the mysterious lure of both the barren
grounds and the desert, the more I come to recognize their
fascination must lie in a special kind of austerity; not in the
sense of a despairing want, but a dispassionate and rigorous
exhibition that the noblest character does not, after all, necessarily lie in affluence but in a truer evaluation of less—a
greater appreciation of what we can use to the best advantage
by wise limitation.

Precipitation, either rain or snow, is not heavy in the arctic.

Scrub timber of the Permafrost region in the arctic forest

Low evaporation from the cold seas lifts little moisture into the air. The total annual fall of moisture in the arctic is generally less than twenty inches. With heavy winds drifting the light fall of snow, a share of the polar area may be free from snow throughout the winter; a sledge might screech over the bare spots like a beaten dog.

The tundra has innumerable shallow lakes that lie on the permafrost. Where the tundra has ample soil, a rather good cover of heather exists, with some fairly high shrubs, but in the sparser soil regions growth is scattered, reminding one of the arid Southwest, where plants survive only when they can arrogate to themselves individual, isolated soil areas and all of the sparsely allocated moisture "within reach." Lichens predominate on the poorest tundra soil, taking their nourishment from the air and dust. Over the regions of solid rock only lichens alone, of course, can grow.

Permafrost (the subsoil permanently frozen) is a condition in the arctic that determines many things. Without it, it is doubtful that most arctic plants would survive at all with such low annual precipitation. In the Southwest desert the incredible yucca sends its roots to unbelievable depths, in some instances down to forty feet, to obtain moisture in a land of little rainfall. Arctic plants to survive would have to do likewise with equally scanty rainfall were it not for the moisture-retaining value of the underlying permafrost. Moisture, being unable to penetrate the frozen ground, is held in reserve near the surface, where a little water goes a long way toward sustaining growth. In both instances of desert and arctic tundra, water utilization becomes an economy miracle—a lesson that might suggest to man a needless, plethoric striving for excess.

When some years back I left Winnipeg, Manitoba, Canada, in February for Hudson Bay by rail, I rode in a modern train with every facility for comfort. The trip from Winnipeg to The Pas, Manitoba, was little different from ordinary, smooth rail travel anywhere. But as the same train left The Pas and wended its way toward Hudson Bay over the permafrost, it slowed down and tossed like a vessel on a sea of swells. Alternate freezing and thawing allows no stability in the laying or maintenance of the track. Thus, through the night I rolled sleeplessly from side to side in the berth of a modern Pullman car, sprawling both arms and legs, trying in vain to sustain a stable position for rest and sleep.

The need for moving the town of Aklavik in the Northwest Territory from its original location of unstable footing is a pointed example of the permafrost condition. The old saying, "Woe to the man who builds his house upon the sand," might better apply to the hazardous lack of underpinning on permafrost. Roads, airfields, and foundations on permafrost seem forever to be threatened, and there is no visible future total solution to permafrost instability.

Even for the arctic summer camper, natural refrigeration is

no problem, though temperatures have reached uncomfortable highs in this land of almost continuous midsummer sun. He can dig a short way into the earth and set-in his grub box on ice. Coolers in the permafrost region have been dug for both domestic and commercial uses. There is little danger of digging through the frost into unfrozen soil, since well-drilling attempts have not yet pierced below the freeze area, which goes as deep as nine hundred feet and more.

In the arctic one can generalize more accurately than when describing most latitude zones in the world farther south, where mountain can be different from mountain and desert from desert. The low temperatures and moderate precipitation of the arctic belt seem to create a zonal condition that is quite uniform, whether it be around one part of the globe or the other. Circumpolar activity, therefore, is much the same for those who explore and study its interesting complexity. The precept here, of course, applies to movement along a particular latitude, not longitude. Obviously, changes north and south in the arctic are apparent, even extreme.

One exception to the circumpolar latitude-uniformity principle—a rather strange exception—is the phenomenon of the Northern Lights, technically and sometimes commonly referred to as Aurora Borealis. This most fantastic and spectacular display occurs with overwhelming beauty and impressiveness through much of the arctic, but strangely not with the same zonal uniformity as other circumpolar phenomena.

Actually, Northern Lights occur throughout the year, but they are most spectacular, obviously, when the sun has moved south and the North lies in the months of darkness. Northern Lights are conspicuous over a wide circular band that extends well down into Canada and over southern Greenland and the northern edge of the Scandinavian Peninsula—but oddly enough, not north of Siberia. If you lay a doughnut-shaped disk down over the area roughly described, with the center of the doughnut's hole at about Thule on the west coast of Green-

A few caribou in the scrub timber of the Barrens

land, the doughnut ring area will indicate the most effective part of the display. In the region suggested by the doughnut's hole, the display, strangely, is not often seen.

Much speculation about the cause of Northern Lights has occurred throughout history—some being novel, humorous, superstitious, or even fabled. Such fables have suggested in certain local regions among natives that vast schools of herring sent off silvery reflections as they turned in unison and flashed their shiny bodies toward the arctic sky. The Cree and some other Indians refer to the Aurora Borealis as *chepuyuk nemehitowuk*—"the spirits are dancing." Now, with less fable but no less romance, scientists have pretty well concluded that the Aurora is due to sun particles traveling at high speed toward the earth, undergoing ionization en route.

Now and then we hear that the fluorescence is so great it actually is audible—a sound comparable to the swishing of silken veils. But even on the quietest arctic night I have not been able to stretch my hearing to this extent. Sound is unlikely if we are to accept the modern, physical explanation of this phenomenon most recently handed down. Yet, if one can perceive the aesthetic value of "color music" as displayed in the Japanese theater, there might be something if only in the *imaginative* play of sound for those who think they hear the Aurora. Here, cold science might dispel too much warm romance.

In the course of my fifty and more years of wilderness travel, changes have come to the North, some, unfortunately, not encouraging. The tragic depletion of the caribou from countless numbers to what is now comparatively more or less a remnant, is a conspicuous and disheartening change. The great caribou migration of earlier days was a spectacle I found worth traveling long wilderness miles by canoe or dog sled to observe. It was a vast, undulating flow, from I could only guess about twenty to fifty miles in width, moving overland for days on end. The reckless slaughter and bad handling of this once great herd is a sad commentary on man's general ecological understanding and his ability to leave alone for his permanent benefit the worldwide natural environment in which from generation to generation he needs to live viably for an eternity to come.

The program for killing off the wolf pack that followed the caribou herd on the spring and fall migration has been a grave ecological mistake. Wolves have proved a healthful complement to the herd, consuming the weak stragglers—thus acting as a constant sustaining element in keeping up the health and vigor of the main herd. The enervation of the caribou herd that followed the destruction of a large part of the wolf pack should have been obvious to anyone having the least capacity for ecological observation. Human hunters, on the other hand, kill largely the healthy animals.

In October the migration of the caribou, though now drastically reduced in numbers, gets under way on the tundra. They move into the subarctic regions of scrub forest and muskeg, returning north again in April. The spring migration always seems to be the most spectacular. It appears then to move in a more systematic mass, although general observations have shown no complete and predetermined annual pattern. Some animals choose to migrate out and away from the central herd, as though belonging to an exclusive set or, perhaps, as one banished. The uncertain time of movement and the route taken meant occasional tragedy in some of the earlier years for exploration parties and for natives, when they waited for the trek of the caribou that failed to appear.

Caribou develop convenient outer sharp rims on their hooves in winter that give a grip on ice, losing the rim of traction in summer. I have often wondered whether this is an adaptive seasonal process in nature or if the rim merely wears off on the rock in summer and grows back when protected from rock friction by snow cover. Whatever the situation, it is a remarkable and most fortunate seasonal coincidence.

An extraordinary geographical aspect of the winter transition from warm latitudes to the white wilderness is that observed by the naturalist C. Hart Merriam. He has shown that the changes in flora and fauna due to latitude are very similar to changes in the flora and fauna due to mountain elevation. For example, as you go from the lower desert region of the Southwest to the region above the timberline in the mountains, various life zones occur, such as Dry-Tropical, Lower Sonoran, Upper Sonoran, Transition, Canadian, Hudsonian, and Arctic-Alpine—altitude changes that are quite favorably equated with latitude changes from the southwestern desert to the arctic. Merriam points up a comparative basic concept that each three hundred miles of latitude change is equal to about one thousand feet of elevation zonal change.

While we no longer live the illusions of early civilization— that if we traveled from the temperate zone far enough south we would burn up, or that if we traveled far enough north we would reach temperatures so frigid they could not be endured by man—we do still entertain some strange and false notions about the Far North climate. We need only consider that temperatures in some parts of the United States occasionally, although not as protractedly, are as cold as those in the arctic, in order to revise our earlier impressions about unbearable human habitation in the regions of the Northern winter.

In Greenland the mountain masses and the ice cap influence the summer temperature along the coast, and so does the ice mass which is stored up through the winter in other polar waters. That the arctic generally should ever need this cooling influence through the summer seems strange to the popular concept that the arctic region is always cold. It can, strange as it may seem, get uncomfortably hot in the arctic. While the arctic midwinter is much in darkness, the midsummer sun at its highest declination beats down on the earth most of each twenty-four hours.

Obviously, where the arctic is concerned, we would be wise to revise most popular concepts.

4

WILDERNESS WINTERING

WINTERING in the wilderness generally begins with a preparation period when there are still a few weeks of mild fall weather and open water for canoe travel. The selection of a site and the building of a winter cabin camp offer many advantages when they can be done before freeze-up. In earlier years, before the advent of much mechanical wilderness transportation, equipment and provisions were moved by canoe to the remote wintering place. Many rivers run out of the wilderness toward canoe embarkation points on the sea. This earlier upstream canoe travel with heavy loads, using only the paddle and tracking lines, was slow. Now, of course, the outboard motor used on a canoe has greatly altered this upstream canoe travel problem, long, comparatively rapid travel against fast water being interrupted only by portages around rapids and falls.

Upstream travel has been accomplished with harness dogs. The canoe was towed or tracked or, in canoe travel vernacular, "lined" upstream by dogs. One still sees this type of towing done, especially by Eskimos on tundra rivers. Lining or towing is a process of attaching one, most often two, lines from the canoe to the harness dogs on shore in such a fashion that the near or shore side of the canoe's bow gets a slight sidewash from the current. By this near-sidewash, the canoe will tack out in the stream, and can be towed if shore obstructions do not prevent it. Where the dogs are not used for lining, they are allowed to run free along the shore. They do a superb job of finding their way through forest, around swamps, over headlands and other rough, obstructive shore country.

What a beautiful sight to travel by canoe below a high, rocky promontory and suddenly see four wolfish-looking malamute dogs standing starkly contrasted against the spruce-studded wilderness sky, eagerly seeking out the canoe. Perplexed to have reached such heights and seeing the canoe at such depth, they seem about to leap from their high position into the water. But high divers they are not, by innate wisdom. As the canoe moves upstream they disappear down the other side of the crest and soon are seen bounding along the shore. Occasionally, they get into a fight among themselves, which necessitates a quick landing of the canoe on a sometimes not too accessible shore to break up such fights, principally to prevent the dogs from seriously hurting or killing one another. At times suturing of their wounds is called for, and a muzzling so they will not chew out the sutures or prolong the fight.

When the lake country of deep bays is reached, a new problem is generally encountered—getting the dogs to follow the shore. After they have had some experience in this, they manage quite well. But at first if a deep bay is crossed with a canoe, the dogs hesitate to skirt the shore, and as a shortcut they try to swim across the bay. Finally, the dogs do learn to skirt the shore of deeper bays. Where bays are too deep and wide, the dogs have to be hauled across the water in the canoe and tethered while a return trip is made for the load.

When hauling-in the winter outfit by canoe, sled dogs become an overly friendly nuisance on the portages. Eskimos have managed to pack small loads on the backs of dogs, but this is a practice used largely when fairly long trips are made overland on bare ground. Over numerous portages it is better to chain the dogs to trees until the load is manually carried over, otherwise the dogs are into everything and can damage food supplies no matter how well protected. I once saw a shipment of ham and bacon lying on the Berens River, Lake Winnipeg, waterfront dock, where the box container made of three-quarter-inch boards had been readily chewed through, the meat neatly carried off.

Since dogs cannot understand their temporary tethering to trees while their owners go off and leave them, they display an aversion to it by every sign of howling dismay. Concluding, no doubt, that they have been abandoned, they give forth with a sad, wailing chorus, yanking desperately at their chain leashes. After a trip or two over the portage, they become a bit confused, seeing one return again and again. At last, they settle down to a snooze with an eye partly peeled for the first sign of release and further action.

Log cabin building in late years has become so refined that when most people think of a winter wilderness camp, they picture a rather major task of supercraftsmanship beyond the average individual's scope. The temporary winter wilderness camp type of cabin, made of logs with the bark on, is no such refined production. It is readily constructed by one man with only an ax, or an ax and a saw, and little or no experience. Since the cabin is not a permanent structure, there is no fancy fitting of corners, no accurate leveling or squaring.

Contrary to the building of a permanent, refined log cabin, the notching of logs in the temporary shelter is done on the upper side of the logs instead of the lower side. Two foundation logs are laid down parallel, placed the proper distance apart for the width of the cabin, and then set reasonably level into the ground a few inches. Rough notches of no particular shape are cut halfway through the logs, about a foot from the ends. The next two logs are then dropped crosswise into these notches and similarly rough-notched; this process is repeated to complete the four walls. All misfit voids created by the notching and the spaces between irregular logs are readily filled with moss. The bark, of course, will be left on the logs.

All of the butts (the thick ends of the logs) are laid toward the front of the cabin for the two side walls. This, as will be seen, will make the front wall higher than the back wall, giving a slope to the side walls and to the roof when it is laid. For the front and back walls, the butts are alternated on every other log as the walls go up, so that they will remain level on top.

The roof consists of forest-cut poles laid side by side, covered with birch or cedar bark or tar paper held down with dirt. Always begin laying the bark or tar paper at the lowest part of the cabin roof, working upward, and lap the bark or tar paper about six inches. This will allow moisture to drain off each layer, as it does from shingles or lapped roofing.

Lumber can be brought in for a door. Better yet, cut slabs from logs for this purpose with a chain saw. The chain saw will likewise provide rough lumber for shelves, door and window frames, even for flooring, unless the dirt floor is used. Heavy cellophane or plexiglass nailed double on a window frame will make a reasonably good window and help to keep it free from frost, or common glass can be used, though more difficult to transport.

When making door and window frame openings, place the completed frame into the opening as soon as possible. Then drive spikes through the frame into the ends of the logs as they go up to support them at this end. The notches, of course, will hold the logs at the other end.

Run the stovepipe through a piece of tin nailed over a hole cut in a wall, or fill the hole with clay around the pipe. Use an elbow on the outside from the horizontal wall pipe to a vertical pipe, and run this vertical pipe at least two feet above the roof, guyed with wire. Pipes put directly through a rough pole-and-bark roof instead of a wall will cause the roof to leak badly. A regular commercial roof jack can be brought in which will permit the pipe to go through the roof, but this will entail careful fitting and tarring of joints, a needless undertaking for the temporary cabin.

There is plenty of work to be done in preparing the winter camp, but when it is spread over about two months of delightful fall weather, it amounts to little more than the physical diversion one enjoys from more sedentary leisure camp interests. With the advent of the chain saw, the tasks of building a cabin, a meat cache, and cutting a supply of winter wood, have become immeasurably easier. The greatest value of the chain saw is that logs can be ripped down the center for half-log, flat surfaces to form floor, window frames, table, shelves, door, benches, and such other items requiring a flat facing. Before the advent of the chain saw, I accomplished this by much labor with an adz or a broad ax—sometimes with only a regular ax. In the wilderness, flat surfaces on which to set something are a convenience taken for granted elsewhere. After weeks of wilderness travel, I find flat surfaces in a cabin on which to set things a conspicuous luxury.

When using the term "easier," as applied to the chain saw, it can and must mean only a higher degree of accomplishment, because a day with a chain saw convinces anyone that it is a tough taskmaster. The saw works faster than its handler desires. Its violent roar and fast cut seem to spur one doggedly on. Since the chain saw motor is often not easy to start, it makes one reluctant to shut it off. Its exhaust noise is never soothing, like the purr of a car motor; rather it is the sound of an intolerant robot gone violently mad. A vast amount of work can, of course, be done with a chain saw in one day, compared to what can be accomplished by handsawing. But I am always glad to have the forest settle down into a more peaceful state after initial work is finished. Wildlife has been sent scurrying to peaceful areas from the first exhaust explosions, and it takes days for the vacuum of wildlife produced by the trip-hammer noise to fill in again.

There comes a day when the cabin is built and the main tasks of preparing for winter are done. Late fall, crisp and invigorating, has by then settled over the forest. Night frosts become regular. The magnificence of golden popple forests against the conifers, splashed in here and there with a mosaic of color from the moose maples, sets off the landscape against the blue autumnal sky and water in a never-failing spectacle. Autumn forest trails are usually moist and silent underfoot. Carpeted with yellow leaves that fall flat and overlapping on the trails, they impart a path-of-gold effect. The forest fragrance is suggestive of firm, ripe apples. To awake in the morning and see a moose calmly feeding in the shallows across the bay is to believe that all, in the final resolution of a troubled world, has gone fairly well—at least it seems so within the compass of one's own wilderness domain.

Not many people, comparatively speaking, have had the priceless experience of long wilderness solitude. Quite often the question is posed, "What on earth do you do up there all winter?" There is no wholly satisfactory answer for those who need to ask. A wide estrangement must inevitably exist between people who find lone hours hanging heavy on their hands and those who fully enjoy the benefits of seclusion and extended leisure. If one must ask what to do with life's most priceless possession—time—perhaps the best answer would be, "If not aware of its inestimable value, sell it to the highest bidder for cash, and always be cheated." As Thoreau said, "No one but a fool ever sold more of his time than he had to."

Hunters and fishermen who in their rush from city to country must continually hunt and fish to ward off boredom should consider Schopenhauer's appraisal of the individual charmed by the myriad forms of natural interest: " . . . boredom," he says, "that spectre which haunts the ordinary man, can never come near him."

No doubt we glorify leisure and long for it more when pressing circumstances continually deprive us of its luxury. The formal, routine demands of urban life have so relieved most people of the need to plan each day and year for themselves, they lose almost completely the sense of individual responsibility and organization in their own lives which could allow leisure. We are generally swept along in a conventional mass, scarcely ever questioning whether the sweeping is with or against the wind of durable human interest—individual or general. After a decade or two of conventionally chained reflexes, there can be only panic for most at the thought of long leisure—say a winter's solitude in the wilderness.

Essentially, life deep in the wilderness has not changed over the years, and in many respects it does not differ intrinsically from our needs anywhere. We must eat, sleep, wear clothes, react intellectually, emotionally, courageously. We live as everyone does universally, with hopes, desires, apprehensions, and we contend with physiological, personal problems and needs, very much as we have always done down through history and continue to do now everywhere in city or wilderness. There are, however, two basic exceptions in the wilderness— repression is vastly diminished, and the opportunity for examining the best of intellectual culture is greatly increased by the proper utilization of leisure time.

Rising from a calm night of fresh air sleep in the unhurried peace of a wilderness cabin is a far cry from the process of dashing cold water into one's face, gulping down a cup of black coffee while standing up, and hurrying through nerve-racking traffic to factory, shop, and office. In the wilderness, the coffeepot gets a place on the wood-burning stove with almost ritualistic ceremony. A small amount of cold water is first mixed with the coffee grounds. Before closing the lid a few

". . . a winter's solitude in the wilderness."

casual inhalations from the pot opening catch the fragrance. Another pot of water is brought to a boil nearby, and then poured into the coffee-cold-water mixture. It is then set far back on the stove to steep. If you like a clear, winelike coffee instead of the mellow mocha and Java blend, you break in an egg or toss in a half teaspoonful of dehydrated egg powder. Soon after the coffee is settled, a substantial breakfast has been prepared in full, and is eaten with deliberate, epicurean delight.

Two windows with double panes of glass to prevent frosting over have been placed in the log walls with consideration for both light and view. One window catches the first rays of morning, the other commands a sweep over miles of frozen lake. Moose, caribou, fox, timber wolves, and other wildlife cross the lake, especially in these early morning hours. The breakfast table is situated so as to embrace a partial view of

The bold Whiskey Jack (Canada Jay)

both areas. Thus, entertainment and the magnificence of a changing panorama of light and shade, created by the low-hanging sun, are a part of every meal.

Dawn does not break or the sun "come up like thunder" over the forest-skirted, snow-covered lakes of the North. The transition from night to dawn is so gradual, one might scarcely know, except by consulting the twilight section of the Nautical Almanac, when the first trace of light should be in evidence. The immaculately white, luminous sweep of snow over the ice is responsible for this vague transition, especially when the moon also diffuses its light with the early rays of the sun. On the other hand, three Whiskey Jacks coming to the feeding station outside the windowsill at dawn announce unmistakably by their presence that daylight is really approaching. Chicka-dees are at the second feeding station, always having to make way for the bold Whiskey Jacks—but they do not seem to mind the preemption. The black-capped chickadee, smaller than a sparrow, with its black bib and white cheeks is the cheerful little acrobat of the North—friendliest of all creatures that glorify man's wilderness habitat. The chickadee seems to

The captivating chickadee

be as much at home upside down as right side up on the suet stations, and as easily takes off into flight from its "pad" whatever position it happens to be holding. It has a very small body, but nature has supplied it with a high body temperature that makes it impervious to the most intense cold, and a deep, downy coat that gives it significant size. Not long after a tent camp or a cabin has been established in the Northern wilderness, the chickadee will, with a little encouragement, feed from one's hand. Its friendly "chick-a-dee-dee" greeting is sounded the moment one steps outdoors. When I fasten crusts of bread to my parka hood, I can feel them pecking away up there.

The chickadee seems to be symbolic of the North. Many northern states and provinces have affectionately wanted to claim it as a state or provincial bird. When the loon became Minnesota's state bird, a trapper preferring the chickadee as a symbol asked, "When my tea pail is hanging over an open fire in a hollow of deep snow—where is the loon? I'll tell you where he is—he's down in Florida shooting off his big mouth!" Not the chickadee; *he* seems as adaptive to his winter environment as the penguin to his.

Whiskey Jack, Gray Jay, Canada Jay, Wiskajon, Lumber-jack, Camp Robber—all these appellations have been be-stowed on this friendly gray bird with white forehead, black patch across the back of the head, and fairly long tail. Larger than a robin, it suggests, as Peterson's bird book reminds us, an enormous, overgrown chickadee. Like the chickadee, the Can-ada Jay seems to enjoy the companionship of people, and no cabin with a promise of food will long be without him.

Water for household use comes from a hole cut in the ice. In Far Northern latitudes this is no small initial task, with ice from three to seven feet thick. Ice chipped from the surface is generally used for water where excessive thicknesses occur. In a forest lake area, once a hole is cut it is protected from freez-ing by covering it with evergreen boughs heaped over with snow, or a cover is made from chain-sawed boards insulated with caribou moss. It is from this hole also that the winter supply of fish might be caught if the depth of the water is sufficient and the hole is situated over a good fish habitat or fishway; otherwise a more selective depth and a more fish-frequented habitat must be found, another hole cut and as carefully maintained. Deep narrows are usually excellent fish-ways, though there are some regions where fishing in narrows is prohibited by law.

Into a water hole in heavy sacks to which lengths of wire are attached go the canned goods, to prevent their freezing during long absences when the cabin is left unheated. Since labels soak off, the cans are marked with wax crayon to avoid having every meal potluck. This storage replaces the traditional root cellar, which is too much of a chore to dig and build into a hillside if the cabin is used only for a single season or two.

Thickening of the ice at freeze-up is watched with some anxiety. As the lakes begin to freeze over, a period of isolation cuts off travel in forest regions but not on the Barrens. One can hike overland in the forest, but this is comparable in ease of mobility to an ant moving through dense grass. Perhaps this isolation is more a condition of mind than actual seasonal entrapment. Yet, one does not escape the feeling that no significant movement will be possible by canoe, dog sled, motorized toboggan, or on foot until the ice thickens or a sudden wind temporarily breaks up the first thin-ice cover. Usually at this time of year a number of prewinter tasks occupy the days in and around the cabin, deferring travel even were it possible. Nevertheless, an unconscious urge keeps plaguing the mind—a kind of frustration at not being able to roam at will.

Some people actually suffer acute feelings of isolation at freeze-up time. Perhaps they are akin to the unreasoned tendency toward claustrophobia.

Inherently, I am a putterer. A half day can be consumed—and profitably, I think—by the most insignificant task. When I am splitting wood, clearing a trail, or performing other heavy physical jobs, I work with fairly consistent energy. But let me refit and work down an ax handle, make a grub box, a pair of snowshoes, a dog sled, repair a canoe, and I get lost in delightful, protracted hours of refining the end result. Much time in the process, of course, goes toward contemplating the immediate natural scene or watching forest creatures. One needs to look up now and then, even from the most absorbing task, in so magnificent a world.

Fortunately, I am endowed with a fair degree of manual sense. Things will take shape for me that inspire a measure of praise, if time is not a pressing factor. When I return to the outside, my equipment is likely to be in better condition than when I entered the wilderness. I am continually intrigued by the necessary correlation between mental and physical activity where human well-being is concerned.

Since two inches of ice has been the common accepted standard for a long time as sufficient to support a team of horses, on this basis one sees fit to travel afoot with a dog sled or motorized toboggan, though ice is still quite thin on lake and river. Some lake shores are shallow enough to risk travel soon after the least supporting ice forms, but in the Precambrian shield of Canada, solid rock headlands frequently rise abruptly out of the water where there are great near-shore depths. Water moving under the ice, whether on lake or river, can create hazardous thin-ice breakthrough spots.

With the advent of the aluminum canoe, a limited amount of travel over thin ice at freeze-up and over decomposing ice at break-up can be done with negligible risk. The method is to place one foot in the aluminum canoe, the other on the ice, hands on the gunwales, and push the canoe along as a youngster would his little express wagon. If alternate open water and float-ice are encountered, half the canoe is run off from the ice into the water. By moving forward in the canoe, it will readily be launched. At the opposite side of the lead or other open water, the canoe bow is run by momentum halfway or more out of the water upon the ice. There a move by the occupant to the front of the canoe will allow footing for pulling it up on the ice. In this fashion it has been possible to avoid isolation during freeze-up and break-up. Wood-and-canvas or all-cedar canoes will not permit this kind of travel without serious attritional damage to the paint and canvas of the canoe. Besides, wood-and-canvas canoes drag sluggishly over snow-covered ice. They can be used in extreme emergency, of course, where canoe damage cannot be considered a factor.

Once firm ice has formed at winter's beginning, travel gets under way in earnest. The cabin will now for a time become only a base of operations. The winter supply of reading material, planned projects of craftsmanship, or other diversions around the cabin lose their immediate importance. They are the interests one returns to after each trip of exploration.

A dozen successive winter tent camps reached by dog team or motorized toboggan intensify the pleasure of being back in the cabin again. At the end of such a trip, one can usually settle down to an extended period of relaxation with only average physical diversion. A sort of domestic bliss ensues.

Even the dogs become resigned to the homecoming and enjoy rest in their cozy, individual houses after their two hundred or more miles of pulling a sled. In time the dogs will again show a restless tugging at their chains for action whenever one leaves the cabin, but now they look rather reproachfully through the corner of an eye, apparently hoping that the harness will not again be slipped over their heads.

Somewhere in the area will likely be an Indian or white trapper. The chances are that he will have discovered your presence before you do his, but not always. His knowledge that you are not usurping his trapping area is all the assurance he needs to welcome you as friend and neighbor, although both of you might have to travel a full day for a visit. Perhaps you will agree to check some of his traps occasionally in the immediate region of your cabin camp when he fails to reach them early enough to prevent fur damage by gnawing rodents and other creatures.

In Canada, trapping areas are now set aside to licensees, a regulation which permits trappers to control catches in their own territory for better propagation. This works several significant advantages. Licensing has stopped much of the reckless competitive trapping which rapidly depleted the fur animals, and has largely prevented the not few violent confrontations and murders that took place when trapping regions were being bitterly contested. Periodical reports required from trappers by the wildlife department prevent, or at least reduce, the depletion of wildlife species and provide more successful conservation programs.

The transistor radio and even the transistor battery-operated TV in some areas have become important entertainment and edification media in the trapper's winter isolation, but I have been deeply impressed by his seemingly greater interest in reading. Thus, we find a number of very well-informed men among them. In my winter wilderness travels when I could make a stop at a trapper's cabin, I have tried to carry whatever packets of books that excess loads over and above camp equipment and provisions would permit on a dog sled. On some of these occasions I felt that I was taking on almost the role of a bookmobile, carrying to a distant trapper the books from a nearer one, and exchanging these for others on the return trip.

Trapping implies bringing industry to the wilderness. To make it profitable is hard and not always fruitful work, despite an expenditure of great physical effort. There are rare winters when fur brings high prices and the catches are big. A light freeze, producing thin ice, followed by a heavy snow, can create a condition which prevents making the complete rounds of a trap line. A wolverine will nevertheless make these rounds, destroying a large amount of fur. The first half of the winter brings the best pelts. Later, the fur may be rubbed off in spots by the animal's travel through brush, burrows, and narrow rock crevasses, giving the hides reduced market value.

The wolverine has probably been one of the trapper's worst enemies. Yet if one admires daring, cunning, and ferocity, here is a creature that deserves admiration. Does he respect and fear the awesome wolf, or any other animal? Let there be several timber wolves far greater than the wolverine's weight and size, devouring a fresh kill. With teeth gnashing, claws swiping right and left, a tempest of flashing violence, the wolverine rushes in to take possession of the kill. There is no actual fight. Wolves, knowing the bellicose nature and fierce fighting instinct of this lesser-sized, muscle-compacted adversary, find it advisable to give ground at once and retreat to a safe quarter. What the wolverine does not eat, he most often spoils with his body excretions.

For many years the trapper has been foiled by the wolverine cunningly springing traps, stealing baits, and destroying catches. But the trapper has at last outsmarted the wolverine by a means so cruel I am reluctant to perpetuate its use by describing it. The wolverine is a natural tree climber. This is

The wolverine—cunning, daring, and ferocious

his undoing. A small tree is lopped off by the trapper as high above the ground as can be reached with saw or ax, a bait placed at the top, and a number of large, barbed fishhooks nailed to the long stump, points upward in such fashion that the wolverine can climb the trunk to get the bait but cannot get down. He is later found cruelly impaled on these hooks, the only mercy being the sub-zero temperatures that take his life as food no longer becomes available to supply body heat. Or the trapper finds the wolverine hung up and shoots him;

and while removing the dead animal, the trapper himself risks being impaled on the same fatal hooks by a slip or careless move.

Before trapping areas were licensed by the government and the trapper was required to report the propagation potential, he too often shortsightedly and competitively trapped every living creature that would provide him with an additional dollar. Regulation of trapping by the wildlife administration is not, I regret to say, to be construed as a completely corrective conservation or ecological measure. It has merely lessened somewhat the former ravage.

All wilderness creatures, no matter how man appraises them for his own benefit, are indispensable to the entire ecological balance of a wilderness. A wilderness region to be broadly functional must be left an inviolate whole. Nothing less than this will do if we are serious about conservation. Deprive a wilderness area of one natural link and you break the ecological chain, upsetting the general pattern, until we have what we see generally after man has sought by artificial measures to "balance" nature—a disconcerting atmosphere of death and barrenness. Eventually, if not too late, man will discover that wilderness areas are ecologically essential to the survival of human life on the globe. Wherever man has sought to regulate wilderness in part or by the concept of "multiple use," it has been wrought with tragic failure.

One or two examples here might illustrate the pattern of our "control" blunders. Since skunks were offensive to man's fastidious notion of a natural environment, man in some areas sought to eliminate or reduce drastically the number of skunks. As a result, the duck population and propagation of many other water birds fell off seriously. This was just "a natural cyclical coincidence," said the conservation authorities. On careful investigation it was found that a big part of a skunk's diet is turtle eggs, which he digs from the sand. Turtles, now relieved of their most ardent predator, multiplying out of all proportion to an ecological balance, were swimming up under the young ducks and other water birds, pulling them under for food in countless numbers.

When this new predation by turtles was realized by conservation authorities, they considered a consequent plan for the systematic destruction of turtles, until it was again shown by a few astute naturalists that here the "conservationist" would upset another balance in nature, and in turn keep upsetting balances successively until the misguided "control" would turn into a kind of wholesale decimation of wildlife. Such tragic meddling has been costing the public vast sums—the money unwittingly used for the destruction of natural resources, not the saving of them.

On another occasion, when all dead trees along a waterfront were cut out to "beautify" it, hawks and similar perching birds living on rodents left the area. As a result, a population explosion of various rodents began to overrun the region until residents along the lake could no longer maintain decorative vegetation around their homes and adjacent farmers lost whole fields of their spring plantings.

And these are only a few of many examples.

We are gradually discovering the infinite resource loss from meddling with nature, but ecological education is tragically slow, no doubt because of its rather abstract nature and man's myopic tendency toward immediate material gain rather than toward permanent and more rewarding values and results. Hiding one ecological blunder with another, man apparently is too confident of his own artificial administration to recognize that the vast and complex process of natural life went on very successfully for countless ages before his "contribution." (We might safely have said, even before his inception.) Man's most valuable experiment in the ecological program so far, though he will not admit it, has been simply "hands off."

CHAPTER

5

WINTER
WITH THE CREE

ALMOST a half century ago, in the northern wilderness of Ontario, I sat as a guest with a family of Cree Indians before an open fire that burned on the ground in the center of a birch-bark tepee. Through the surrounding Precambrian region of lakes and largely coniferous forest, the accumulated snow of months lay from four to five feet on the level—drifting even higher here and there on the lake shores and in the small forest openings, wherever the wind had access. Seven sled dogs nearby, all part wolf—three my own team—had burrowed into the soft snow to escape the February cold. They were individually chained a safe distance apart from one another to keep the peace.

Here in the wilderness I had at last come to the focal point of a long-awaited interest. Any plausible or concrete reason I might offer for being here would be only an affected justification. Restlessness from the enervating supercomfort of city life had been gnawing away at me for months. This, I am sure, could be interpreted by some as nothing more than the common, on-the-go urge of callow youth to be some place other than where he is. Be this as it may, on looking back I must confess that if maturing years tend to offer a cure for itineracy, the clinical effects of time on me have failed utterly.

Days by rail and nearly a week of lone dog sled travel were required to reach these people whom I had met during the previous season's canoe travel on the Berens River, Manitoba. The greatest task in the trek was that I had to search for their nomadic camp in a vast wilderness, though I had been given a general clue as to their whereabouts.

Here in the Northern forest I found life pretty well unencumbered, reduced to the barest essentials. Henry David Thoreau summed it up very well when he said that we need to strive for simplicity as the most important advantage in life, and do our bookkeeping on our thumbnails.

All of us, including the dogs, had just eaten our fill of moose meat. Closer to the truth, we had gorged ourselves on it almost to a state of torpor. Reclining on woven rabbit-skin sleeping robes, cushioned by more than a foot of evergreen boughs, we proceeded socially to drink unbelievable quantities of tea, while a young Indian lad who had been off to mission school acted as interpreter to penetrate the existing language barrier as we swapped stories and trail talk.

Needless to say, I, too, at my age was picking up some of the Cree language. Each detail of the Indian camp, its accouterments, its people, was being etched on my mind—betraying an eagerness for romance that must always, I suppose, be the enviable prerogative of impressionable youth.

The birchbark tepee occupied by these natives was of double construction to a point well above the snow line, insulated between with dry caribou moss—in all, a marvel of fine Indian craftsmanship. When my host explained that the insulation was primarily to prevent the snow from melting against the

"The birchbark tepee—a marvel of fine Indian craftsmanship."

heated birchbark wall, preserving in turn the even greater insulating value of the snow, I realized that technology of this sort was ages old and could not be considered the special prerogative of an industrial age.

Smoke had been drifting lazily out over the spruce forest from the peak of the tepee. There, ingenious flaps controlled by a long pole from the ground handled the draft as the wind changed. Yet, in spite of this control, a stratum of smoke hung just above our heads as we sat on our rabbit-skin robes spread over the bough-covered floor. At first, I gave no particular heed to the suspended smoke. In fact, I thought it rather fragrant—except, I might add, for a secondary, obtrusive "high" odor of drying fur pelts. A time came, however, when my eyes began to smart, and not being a user of tobacco, the smoke also irritated my throat. Years previously, on an extensive dog sled journey, I had suffered from a case of snow blindness— the early symptoms being comparable to what I was now beginning to feel.

To endure the irritation, I slumped down on my elbows to a lower level of less-smoke-filled air, but this was not enough. Uneasily, I sought a solution—a dozen ideas flitting through my mind—as I tried to hide my increasing discomfort. Inured to tepee smoke through successive winters, the Indians seemed to endure it with incredible tolerance—another envy among many others that were plaguing my youthful desire to emulate the elemental and Spartanlike simplicity of these people.

The elder of the family, observing my low-level crouch, smiled compassionately. "Even the Indian," he said through our young translator, "knows the pain of tepee smoke when the wind will not carry it off. As one grows very old it is better maybe to be warm and have the smoke, than be cold and have the good air."

As he spoke, a timely recollection occurred to me.

"There are a people in a far-off land across the big water," I explained, "who live in hogans and herd many reindeer—a very cold land where fires are built on the ground in the middle of the hogan floor. The people are called Lapps." (With the terse term *Cree* in mind, it seemed propitious to shorten Laplanders to Lapps.)

"Because the country is very cold," I went on, "the hogans have to be made very tight, and this would make them fill up badly with smoke. The Lapps know they must somehow bring air from the outside into their hogans, so they dig and cover a trench in the ground from the outside under the wall of their hogans to the underside of the fire. The fire is then built over a rock opening at the end of the trench. Air works its way through the trench, is heated as it passes through and around the fire making the fire burn brighter. In this way, there is always fresh air in their hogans."

With gestures across the tepee floor, I simulated the construction of the Lapps' device to move air by convection from the outside of the fire. The entire family listened intently. I paused between each sentence to wait for my interpreter's translation.

More than anything, the Indian loves a story, either true or legendary.

Of the Lapps, these Indians knew nothing, yet the tale caught their fancy. Whether or not the prospect of ridding their tepee of smoke was welcomed, they showed no immediate expression of approval or disapproval. Could it be that I had offended them with this tale—a disparagement of their gracious hospitality?

Whatever their inward reaction, I concluded that I could not tolerate the smoke through the night. In my mind I sought every devious device for escape, succeeding eventually but with questionable grace. Unlashing my winter camping gear from the toboggan, I proceeded to set up a camp in a nearby grove of balsams.

By custom I was expected to spend the night in the tepee of my hosts. My sleep consequently was disturbed by that usual indisposition one suffers from worrisome thoughts. Despite trail fatigue and a comfortable bed, I lay sleepless.

A backdraft device in the vent pipe of my "airtight" kept the tent at a comfortable temperature, and of course, smokeless.

My field thermometer, hanging from a nearby branch outside the tent, reached 41 degrees below zero at bedtime. The lake, at intervals, gave out a low-pitched, thundering *carrr-oom!*—temperature fissures miles long being ripped by the cold in the vast stretches of the lake ice.

I could hear a small creature of some kind outside my tent, perhaps a weasel or mink, brush against the exterior wall. It seemed to be sniffing out this strange new addition to the Indian camp. Once, deep in the forest, there came the pitiful cry as of a baby, and I knew that a snowy owl had likely swooped down on a hapless snowshoe hare. The sled dogs stirred restlessly during the owl escapade. I heard them emitting a few half-interested feeble howls, soon settling down again into their snowy beds. In a snug winter camp I always suffer compassion for the dogs who must sleep in the snow.

Those who loosely boast that sled dogs can sleep comfortably in the snow with no ill effects should revise this belief. I have come to know better. Many sled dogs become hopelessly crippled from rheumatism. At one time, for almost a hundred miles, I carried on my toboggan a rheumatically crippled lead dog wrapped in my sleeping robe. In the tent, I warmed her near the stove for hours, spoke soothing words, and hourly rubbed her stiffening body. I gave her warm food and every possible care for a week. Then finally I had to carry her off into a hidden section of the forest away from the other dogs and with my Winchester carbine relieve her of her misery.

When on such a day the realities of the trail became grimly evident, they seemed almost to fall in numbered sequence. I was at that time desperately short of feed for the dogs. There was but one choice. I met it the most practical way, by cooking her and feeding her to her mates. For a time I felt disturbed, but this did not seem relatively quite as difficult, I later found, as the killing of one healthy, devoted dog after another for food to keep myself alive.

Sometime during the night as I lay semi-sleepless in my own

camp near the Indian tepee, I heard the wind rise. The temperature also was rapidly rising from an earlier minus 41. I nevertheless refueled the stove for the remaining portion of the night, then untied enough tapes in the tent flap openings to peer out. My suspicions were correct. Driving snow raced past the tent opening with the sound of white-water rapids.

I could hear the wind wrestling even with the well-protected, deep-in-the-forest balsam grove around my tent. There was a secondary sound from the direction of the lake—a kind of muffled, spasmodic thumping as the wind roared through and over what seemed to be an obstacle course of forest barriers, as though maddened by these obstructions. In meteorological terms, or in fact by any standard, this was a blizzard.

Sometime in the course of the night my trail-weary body must have subdued my mind, for I did not awake until well after dawn. In the short days of the Northern winter, dawn means a late hour. By now, the blizzard had settled down to a steady, howling progression, whirling the snow with relentless fury into every forest void. But the full sound effect of it was not felt in the tent, and I eventually learned why. Snow had drifted up almost to the tent ridge, and my stovepipe was projecting scarcely a foot above the shifting snow's crest. I had, in short, along with the double-tent principle, been protected by a "snowdrift igloo," wholly impervious to the blizzard that raged. Warmed by nature's insulation and a wood fire, my comfortable situation could briefly be described as "cozy."

Since most Indians prefer tea to coffee, no overtures were necessary toward having a sociable breakfast. By melting snow I soon had that exquisite aroma pervading the tent—coffee! I fried a generous moose-meat steak in bacon fat and made a modest-sized, raisin-filled bannock on the stove, preceding this with some apricots which I had stewed during the early, sleepless part of the night. It was a real day-starter breakfast. In the city my breakfast usually consists of a small glass of orange

juice, a three-minute egg, a single piece of toast, and a generous amount of coffee. Once, while in a lumberjack town, I
ordered such a breakfast. A big, burly lumberjack seated at the
counter beside me, devouring an enormous breakfast of
cooked cereal, pancakes, ham, eggs, and potatoes, looked at
my modest fare, then bent over toward me and whispered,
"Say, Buddy, if you're a little short, I'll stake you to some
grub."

The storm carried well into the second day. During my confinement I took the opportunity of reading Thoreau's *Walden* a
second time. It was a copy from which I had ripped the hard
cover to save weight on the trail. Gradually, toward night of
the second day, the storm abated. Morning of the third day
broke with a sun as glaring as the summer desert's. The beauty
of sun-splashed new snow and the coniferous green of the
forest under a blue sky was a dazzling, incredible spectacle. I
had stayed pretty much to myself during the storm, except to
feed the dogs and provide balsam-bough protection for them.
My Indian friends had slumped into a kind of lethargy of semi-
hibernation during the storm—a condition I have seen practiced among Eskimos, but not to any apparent degree among
Indians.

When I heard considerable activity around the Indians'
tepee after the storm, I broke my isolation and made a snowshoe trail to their tepee, hurdling enormous drifts as I made
my way. None of the Indian family showed the slightest evidence of offense toward my camp isolation during the storm. I
cut wood, tended the dogs, and made myself useful without
appearing unduly solicitous. I had somehow fallen into the
good graces of these people (not always an easy thing to do),
and my mind once again was at ease.

Apparently, the story of the Laplanders' method of getting
rid of smoke in their hogans became an important topic of
conversation throughout the blizzard, for they broached the
subject rather directly at the first opportunity. It is doubtful,

however, that they suffered any smoke irritation during the
howling blizzard, since the draft at the apex of the tepee must
have been greatly increased.

The ground inside the tepee already being thawed from the
heat of continual fires, we split out and hewed with an ax
several wood paddles to dig a narrow trench, succeeding without any difficulty in the area from the fire to the birchbark
wall. But just outside the tent where we needed the fresh air
opening into the trench, we ran into solidly frozen earth. To
thaw the ground without burning down the tepee became a
special problem. Finally, we accomplished it by starting the
thaw-fire well away from the tepee, keeping the fire deep in a
trench as the ground thawed toward the tepee.

The mother of the Indian family supplied the birchbark to
cover the fire-to-wall trench inside the tepee. At first I thought
this would present a problem, with birch trees frozen hard as
bone. However, great rolls of birchbark were dug from deep in
the snow—surplus bark left from the previous fall when the
tepee was built. After covering the trench with this bark, sticks
were laid across the birchbark for support, then balsam
boughs, covering all within a short distance of the fireplace.
The final problem was posed when we needed flat stones to
continue the trench into the fire area and also for creating the
fireplace itself.

Stones there were no end of on this Precambrian, rocky
lake shore, but where to look under about five feet of snow?
Again the mother solved the problem. She remembered exactly
where the outside summer fireplace of flat stones had been
laid. With snowshoes as shovels, and a great deal of hilarity, all
of us proceeded to dig. Snow flew gaily from the spot. The sled
dogs, failing to understand the excitement, and now overrested
because of the storm, tugged at their leashes and howled—anxious to join the commotion. A fire was needed to loosen the
stones from their frozen earth bonds when at last we did reach
them.

With enough stones finally assembled, we managed to complete the experiment, and at once laid a fire. By convection, the air from outdoors moved freely through the trench into the stone-housed, fireplace area and caught the fire with a fine, liberal draft, sending its cheery glow upward with an active, bright flame. The test would soon come as the smoke accumulated overhead. For a few moments it started to form a stratum, and I began to suffer qualms both for the reputation of the Lapps and myself. But as the smoke reached the apex of the tepee, suddenly a natural draft was formed. Air replacement swept the smoke through the apex opening and carried it off with complete success as a continuing supply of fresh air, warmed by the fire, moved the smoke upward and out. The fire, with ample air for combustion, now also burned brighter and more cheerily. The law of physics was having full play.

"Sakaputao!" ("The smoke rises!"), exclaimed the Indian mother as she started to prepare a celebration feast. She was proclaimed the chief expediter of the whole event, which made her chuckle with hearty laughter—not fully sure what the adulation for her was all about.

Joy came into the camp. The smoke curse would no longer lower the spirits of these Indians through the prolonged Northern winter. The wisdom of the Lapps had crossed the ocean to brighten the world of the Cree.

6

REMITTANCE MEN
AND OTHERS

As one travels winter wilderness trails, visits to those who lead isolated lives are not confined to trappers alone. Unlike the trapper, the most eccentric and intriguing individual is the man who has removed himself to some remote wilderness spot for an obscure reason which most often he keeps to himself.

Most of us have heard of the so-called remittance man—the eccentric who did not fit into a status-seeking, affluent family in England—the traditional black sheep. Pomp and material splendor, social affectation, or even unaffected, normal social life—these bored him to a point of indignation and revolt. Generally the most logical recourse left to his family was to give him an annual stipend if he would depart for one of the colonies an ocean away and remain there beyond the need of continual family apology for his disturbing, unconventional conduct.

He is not always, of course, the rebellious sophisticate who is

". . . visits to those who lead isolated lives are not confined to trappers alone."

in conflict with social formalities. At times, he is irascible and even criminally delinquent. But this incorrigible type usually drifts to the cities, practicing crime or becoming a victim of alcohol.

The remittance man you find in the wilderness is usually of a different stripe. He may settle in a cabin at the fringe of an outpost settlement, or he is just as apt to be found in the far wilderness, where he will "hole up for the winter," grub-staked, housed in a rough, picturesque log cabin on the shore of a magnificent body of water. He will be well stocked with reading matter; and today, articulate enough to avail himself of a transistor radio or even a battery-operated television set. In most instances, he lives as independently as he can possibly arrange his insular existence without repression or need of austerity. Taxes, social obligations, community responsibility, or any of the other numerous institutions of involvement that press as duties on the conventional man, he avoids without guilt, qualms, or arrogance.

By the very nature of his general temperament and unconventional leaning, he seems to love wilderness life. This, I have to assume, is not the sole reason for his isolation, if there can or ever need be a categorically sound reason. Life in the winter wilderness, while it implies an expenditure of physical energy, is, of course, comparatively easy with a small budget. In fact, a bigger income, strangely enough, would contribute little more to the remittance man's general welfare. It might even prove a hindrance, since he gratifies his desires largely through the enjoyment of natural tasks of daily living: fishing and hunting for food, travel, reading, even, occasionally, the creation of literature or art.

Intellectual pursuits are not anomalous in wilderness life, for remittance men have been generous contributors to the world's literary and artistic treasure—often anonymously, more often by pseudonym.

Housing, water, fuel, meat, fish, berries, diversion, amusement, and a number of other incidental advantages are largely free in the wilderness, his for the taking. Consider, if you will, these essential items in the urban man's total winter budget and you have accounted for the expenditure of most of his income. Thus, in the wilderness the remittance man has found by the most natural selection a living area of least imposing demand, with the added luxury of leisure.

It would be wrong to suggest that the remittance man dislikes people generally and, like a hermit, is able to maintain a wholly nongregarious life. None of us can be considered a hermit by nature, although I have known a few who seemed close to being likely exceptions. We scarcely need to consider remoteness anymore with our modern-day travel facilities of planes equipped with skis or pontoons, of outboard-motor craft and motorized toboggans. Most remittance men I have known lived within a reasonable day's travel, or less, from a settlement or an Indian encampment, by virtue of such equipment or even before these modes of transportation.

Some have a highly refined log or frame cabin, and not infrequently a white or Indian mistress. A woman living with a man in a cabin in the wilderness can suggest a housekeeper, or whatever designation you wish to attach to her capacity. But few will consider that only domestic services are required from a woman occupying a remote cabin with a man—especially if you appraise his selection.

A young Indian girl living in a cabin without wedlock explained to an Indian agent, "I got one blanket, he got one blanket; too cold sleep one blanket." And so, extenuating circumstances make some unions plausible, even valid, in the elemental life of the silent places.

Perhaps, as indicated, one lives closer to natural or more primal reality in the wilderness. At least, convention and pretentiousness become more remote, if not wholly obscured. I have never known the Provincial Police or the Royal Canadian Mounted Police of Canada, for example, to interfere with a compromising situation between a man and a woman living out the winter in a wilderness cabin, unless some meddling puritanic pressure was brought to bear on them.

An Indian girl living with a white trapper of my acquaintance was reported by a missionary to the Indian reservation elders, who advised the trapper he would have to marry the girl or she must leave. She left, and that temporarily ended the episode. Soon the same situation was repeated and continued for several winters until finally it was ignored. The couple eventually were married without outside provocation or approval of any kind.

An Indian trapper friend of mine in Ontario, a man of fine physical stature and mind, met an attractive, village-bred Indian girl when he arrived at the outpost to sell his furs. After a week of courtship, he proposed marriage. She accepted, but told him that she had to make some special arrangements first and needed money. Much of the trapper's winter catch went to complete these "arrangements." He returned time and time again throughout the year, but no marriage was forthcoming. When he arrived the following season with his trapping stake, she made it clear to him that she would marry him, but apparently there were still more "arrangements" to consider. He left a modest sum with her and marked time.

The police were called in on several occasions to quell heated arguments between the two in the local tavern. Thus, the police became all too familiar with the situation. Later in the winter when the trapper reached the outpost to claim his bride-to-be, again she needed more money for "arrangements." This time her ruse to filch a few more dollars failed.

The following day it was reported to police that an Indian girl was being manhandled on the settlement street. The girl was virtually being wrestled in high argument toward the frozen shores of the waterfront a half mile from the wilderness settlement. There at the shore she was bundled into caribou robes in a carriole type of dog sled and apparently tied down, while the police, wise in knowledge and judgment of this romance, saw wisdom in ignoring the episode.

Six months later, the couple reappeared at the post for a marriage ceremony. The interim had been, if not amicable, then fruitful, but it did also seem that the relationship had grown somewhat more compatible. As the police saw them pass down the street, one officer was overheard to have said, "What a man!" The other replied, "And, if you haven't noticed, what a woman!"

In the remote wilderness, one approaches an unknown cabin with some reservation. Years ago, I drew up with a hand-hauled toboggan and a light winter camp outfit at a cabin about three days' travel from the Canadian National Railway in Ontario, the location of the cabin having earlier been pointed out to me on the map. Some unknown "recluse," as he was referred to, had been living there for several winters, the subject of much gossip and conjecture, until the mystery about him was so shrouded it became a sort of backwoods legend. I had been pulling my own toboggan load over a long trail, and when late in the day I arrived near the cabin, I was ready to welcome any reasonable offer of hospitality. Smoke was rising lazily from the chimney.

Any concern I might have had about hospitality was needless. A very personable man of athletic build, apparently in his thirties, beckoned me inside even before I had time to introduce myself. Coincidentally, he was making coffee on a wood-burning stove and turned to it with routine nonchalance, serving me as though I had reserved the preparation of it for my arrival.

"What a pleasant coincidence!" I remarked.

"No coincidence," he assured me. "I saw you coming miles away." The cabin here had an expansive view of the lake.

We measured each other critically though nonchalantly across the coffee table. I have learned not to be overly solicitous and gabby under such circumstances.

The cabin of logs with bark on showed no particular building skill, but it was substantial and comfortable. Corners were crudely notched—any roughness of ax work readily compensated for by a liberal chinking of moss. On the gable-end walls overhead were wide, thirty-inch shelves of rough poles, laid side by side, reaching from side wall to side wall, where, uniquely, storage did not usurp any of the floor or other living space. A table from hand-hewed boards looked thoroughly scrubbed. It held the customary complements for a wilderness coffee break: a No. 2½ tomato can, serving as a sugar bowl, and a can of condensed milk with two nail holes punched in the top—one hole for pouring, the other as an air intake for free flow of milk. A bookcase, also made from hand-hewed boards, held at least a hundred books, but I was then too far away from them to read the titles. Later, examining them, I concluded that here must be a sophisticated individual with intellectual leanings.

I broke the ice of reserve by suggesting that I belonged to the same school of milk-can openers as he did; that my partner of many trips into the wilderness insisted on opening a can of milk with a trail ax, rather than punch with a nail two neat, small holes that would keep out dirt and bugs as well as prevent the milk from drying out.

Question Number 1, unasked: "What is this man doing here alone in the Canadian wilds?"

Question Number 2, unasked: "How do I go about dramatizing my conversation with a naturalness that will be proof to an intelligent man that I have no intention of prying into his affairs, even though I am smarting with curiosity?"

Question Number 3, unasked: "How can I make my purpose for being in the wilderness clear without indicating that since I had revealed my own identity and purpose it is an open invitation for him to lay bare his life?"

Observation Number 1: He has a British accent. (Most Canadians sound pretty much like Americans.)

Observation Number 2: He has made no overtures toward asking my purpose for being in the wilderness; therefore, judging by his innuendo of noncommitment, he must be planning to hide his reason, if he could possibly need one, for being here.

Observation Number 3: Already, I think, he has committed himself to putting me up for the night. But, no doubt, he wonders how long I will obtrude upon his seclusion and hospitality.

It began to snow.

Large fluffy flakes fell almost perpendicularly past the window in front of the coffee table. We now had a subject in common—the weather. I was somewhat relieved to think that it was not a special prerogative of conversation belonging only to one of us.

Using the snowfall as another vehicle of conversation to gain intimacy and relieve the social strain, I began narrating to him the story of the two mountaineers living together in a cabin far from voices other than their own. They had exhausted most mutual subjects. As they rose on a particular morning it was snowing hard. One remarked, "It is snowing." Six or more hours passed and it was still snowing. Nothing having been said all day, the other mountaineer remarked, "Look at it now." Silence from then on until the next morning when one remarked, "It is still snowing." The second mountaineer, "I guess we talked that over pretty well yesterday."

As we visited into the night, I found that a moat of estrangement existed between my host and me, wider than the water separating Canada and the British Isles. This gap seemed to narrow somewhat when I suggested that he put his bedroll on the toboggan in the morning and we travel together. He did not respond, though I thought he looked receptive. Over breakfast the following morning, without further invitation, he agreed to accompany me. For three weeks we pulled that toboggan and outfit over a share of Ontario's lake and portage trails, exploring various wilderness prospects of interest and developing a fine friendship that has been long-enduring.

He proved not to be a remittance man in the full, common sense of the term. He was able by pretense, at least, he told me, to make a conventional adjustment to the banality of a stiff, social-minded English family, but he could not, he pointed out particularly, find his forte in the office confinement of English industry. He was one of four sons. Thus, no problem existed where a junior ascendancy to the business management was needed should his father give way to retirement. Apparently, the father, a generous-minded man deprived of a fuller life by industry, a family, and his wife's social calendar, saw adventure in his son's eyes, and with a remittance arrangement, enviously wished him bon voyage as he left England's shores. It is not the first such instance, to be sure, where parents, being denied the opportunity for adventure themselves, vicariously enjoy it through their offspring.

Men take to the wilderness for many reasons. Matrimonial problems are not the least. Criminals, some with extenuating circumstances that might be condoned, also have lost themselves in the wilds.

In the mountains of Montana, I came upon a recluse whose wall of secrecy was maintained until death. He lived an unobtrusive life of prospecting, gardening, hunting, and fishing. At the time, I was a cowhand in the Musselshell River country.

As winter began to break, I had restored an abandoned log cabin in the Crazy Mountains, and planned to winter there with a companion cowhand. We were not familiar with the region except the area adjacent to the cabin and the route east along the Musselshell. Sometime after we had become settled in our winter cabin camp, we noticed snowshoe tracks that were not our own, and decided to follow them. After a rather long trek, we found that the tracks led to a well-secluded cabin. Whenever we tried to visit the place, the occupant's fresh snowshoe tracks invariably led off into a canyon. This happened too often to be coincidental. On one occasion we were fairly certain on seeing the pattern of snowshoe tracks that he was still in the cabin, but no answer came to our knock on the door. (Whenever I personally did not want company at my own cabin, I would walk away on snowshoes, then reverse them front to back, and return to the cabin. This gave the illusion of two people having departed from the cabin.)

Years later, after I had left the cattle country, a letter reached me from my Montana companion, stating that the mountain recluse had died in his cabin—alone. When authorities examined his personal effects, including some old newspaper clippings, it was learned that he was a fugitive in an out-of-state murder case. Also, that the unearthing of a buckskin poke containing a small amount of gold caused treasure seekers to dismantle the entire cabin and dig up the surrounding grounds for possible hidden gold from his prospecting. Their efforts at thievery and vandalism, however, proved futile.

Allegedly, in his early days, this recluse had been in a gunfight during a poker game. He had, in a sense, been hiding, and kept himself socially elusive all the rest of his life. Prying into this man's former life was no business or plan of my companion or mine, not through a lack of curiosity but largely because it was not generally a common practice in those days to inquire into a man's past—it was "un-Western," so to speak. Had we been able to meet with him, and had he trusted our motives in so doing, we could, no doubt, have offered and enjoyed a winter of mutual sociability. Apparently, he dared not risk the hazard of allowing anyone even a fleeting glance over his wall of secrecy.

As our winter trails lead to the cabins of men living serene lives, or those living in "quiet desperation," we are invariably left with a reflective mood. A strange aspect seems to shroud the lone individual escaping from his plight to the deep wilderness. Comfort he has, and exclusion which he needs for defense against society's immutable passion for revenge, social obtrusion, encroaching economic pressures, and a hundred other potential hazards to his mind and body. When I see the rising drifts of snow and hear the mournful wind in the conifers around the wilderness cabin of a remittance man or other recluse, it seems that he has, as it were, ritualistically foresworn the attributes of a conventional world and donned the monastic robes of an unknown faith.

A popular question arises: Would these people who seek remoteness, as remittance men or otherwise, continue their lives of solitude should they suddenly be endowed with substantial financial means? I guided a banker and his attorney at one time over a wilderness trail by dog team to a remote

mountain cabin. Here lived a prospector. His finds for many
years had been small and sporadic, but at last a major success
had come his way. He was to be advised on our visit that his
recent mineral findings were sold at a substantial sum; that
there were papers to sign, with an accompanying check which
would leave him financially independent.

After several days' travel, we arrived at his cabin, set snugly
in a mountain fold, near a fantastically iced-over waterfall.
There we found the prospector methodically splitting wood.
The wood splitting seemed routine because he already had a
woodshed well stocked with short, stove-length splits.

He took the good news of his prospecting success with little
more than mild pleasure. Over coffee and some delicacy food
items we had brought along, the suggestion was made that the
prospector accompany us back to the city where a little celebration might be in order. Politely, he declined. As we left, he
followed us outside and waved farewell. At an elevation on our
trail we looked down into the mountain fold and saw that he
had returned to his woodshed. Soon we heard the methodical
thud of his ax as he continued to split wood.

How often since have I not considered the true impact of
this lesson upon life's essential values. As a graduate mining
engineer, this prospector had the sophistication to be well in-
tegrated with the outside world, had he so chosen. In later
years when I visited him, I could not see that his added security had in any apparent way altered his gracious approach
to an unaffected, natural, and serene life. I asked him if his
success and means did not change somewhat his former situation and outlook. (He had made subsequent mineral finds and
sold them.)

"I prospect now," he said, "for life's more durable pleasures."

7

INCREDIBLE
NATURALISTIC MAN

THIS chapter, to be conventionally acceptable, should, perhaps, make a distinction between "civilized" man as contrasted to "savage" or "primitive" man. Derogatory terminology commonly applied to wilderness-living people has irked many of us, largely because it closes too many doors of knowledge to the aspiring student of ethnic science and defers fact to false conception. In this chapter, therefore, I prefer to make the distinction between "industrialized" man and "naturalistic" man.

A careful study of the Franklin Expedition and some others —with duly recognized exceptions—should point up the common misconceptions regarding the Eskimo. Sir John Franklin and his entourage, with the highest standard of industrial equipment available at that time, perished to the last man in an area where the Eskimo routinely maintained a viable existence. During the winter in the area where Franklin and his men were decimated by starvation, cold, and scurvy, Eskimos in the same general region, unaided by rifles and other modern equipment of the Franklin party, not only were free from scurvy, but were living off the country on a balanced diet, were procreating, raising their children, maintaining a high degree of social contact, enjoying entertainment, ceremony, and otherwise carrying on life through the arctic winter.

We may assume that had Franklin been able to subordinate his military pomp and disdain of Eskimo acumen, the expedition members, by imitating the Eskimo's methods, might at least have survived. The point here, I think, is not too far-fetched. People who lack intellectual humility generally are destined to lose the fruits of outstanding achievement.

John Rae, a man who recognized and adopted the expedient naturalistic values and accomplishments of the Eskimo, within a decade of the Franklin Expedition wintered successfully in the same area. So did Vilhjalmur Stefansson and others who, by recognizing Eskimo competence and skills, maintained themselves well and eventually completed extraordinary exploration objectives. Many of us, I might add, who have traveled in the Northern wilderness have succeeded largely by enjoying a community of decency with natives and a respectful, advantageous study of their crafts.

The Eskimos learned down through the centuries that by eating all edible parts of an animal, including those in the commonly considered "inferior" category, a nutritional balance was maintained. Vitamin C—the lack of which was the chief difficulty in the dietary problem of early exploration—*is* found to be adequate when all edible parts of an animal are consumed. Officers of some expeditions, who ate only "select cuts," were usually the first to suffer scurvy, spitting out their teeth with every ill-advised command.

While Eskimos consumed the entire edible portion of the animal killed, they also ate the partly digested vegetable matter in the animal's intestines—a sort of "salad"—to obtain nutritional balance. Whether Eskimos actually *knew* the importance of certain food is a point on which we can only speculate, but in dietary practice, they have managed for ages what we failed to achieve until a comparatively short time ago.

To the discovery of vitamin deficiency and its correction, we as "industrialized" man quickly attach a scientific determination. Where these nutritional discoveries or uses have been the "naturalistic" man's long before white man knew about them, we treat this in scientific and conventional circles as "instinct" or "natural selection,"—thus deviously obscuring fortuitousness or accident in white man's development and obscuring creativeness in "naturalistic" man's.

In our tendency to be derogatory and facetious where naturalistic man is concerned, it may be a revelation to those who slurringly refer to the Eskimo as existing on blubber, that fat provides only a balanced part of his meat diet—about 1 of fat to 7 of lean meat—less fat than consumed by industrialized man with his bacon, fresh pork, full-marbled beef, butter, cream, milk, eggs, cooking and frying fat, candy, cake, ice cream, pie, cookies, suet puddings, and pastries. Since the fat in most of these exist in culinary disguise, the quantity of fat consumed is far in excess of what is ordinarily realized.

A rather substantial amount of fresh vegetable matter comprised the early and now present Eskimo's fare. The gathering and drying of berries was and is common among them. A number of edible seaweeds, rich in minerals, are used. A tuber called Eskimo potato along with plants of the vetch family are common and are prepared through the winter with meat. Some Eskimo tribes for centuries have consumed from 5 to 50 per cent vegetables in their diet, all of wild origin. Now, of course, they purchase some commercial foods in those areas accessible to supply posts. Thus, we can afford to abandon our disparaging concept of the Eskimo, along with a vast amount of other racial misinformation which we so glibly circulate for our own comparative exaltation.

". . . an elemental, naturalistic life in . . . the arctic archipelago . . ."

In this same vein, a common misconception is that the Eskimo suffers bitter conflict with the elements and undergoes a desperate struggle for human existence. Well, what is an Eskimo? I know one who operates several large seacraft along the coast for trade with a big financial investment. A short time ago I visited villages on Hudson Bay. A number of Eskimos there live in modern cabins with bathrooms and up-to-date kitchens. Some Eskimos punch clocks, work on the Dew Line, teach school, give daily radio broadcasts, and carry on other projects. Others, of course, do live an elemental, naturalistic life in the arctic wilderness, the interior barrens, along the coasts of the Northern mainland and the arctic archipelago, with a viability that baffles most of us.

Both Eskimos and Indians look upon white man's day-in and day-out industrial addiction as a tragic incursion upon leisure. Both Eskimo and Indian, where steadily employed, take much time out for the naturalistic life—the hunt, the ceremony, the diversion—and consequently create the impression of irresponsibility. Wisely, they show a greater responsibility to leisure and life.

When Aristotle 2500 years ago suggested that the purpose of education is to teach man how to live rather than how to earn a living, he no doubt had in mind even in that day the moderating of industrial obsessionism, which the naturalistic man seems to understand better than the sophisticate of today —a lesson that the sophisticate will some day have to learn before he can eliminate many of his modernization ills.

Another example of the alleged but false disparity between industrialized and naturalistic man is shown by the great facility the Eskimo has for making and handling tools—especially those he made and used in his earlier, natural life. As the Eskimo later adopted the white man's factory-made tools, he has shown the white man's common manual adeptness in the handling of them. I watched an Eskimo dismantle an outboard motor and assemble it without previous training, something which, of course, might occur anywhere with any race.

The mistake I am perhaps making here is to suggest that ethnic differences might have something to do with skill, ability, and intelligence. I have not found this true. I point up the Eskimo's position primarily to suggest that he is not basically different, except culturally, from any other race. If our investigation into Eskimo life could be based on the general premise that little difference exists between races of men, we could cover a vast area of research into man's problems and potentials without redundant study of ethnic negligibles. Culture and long habit are, obviously, highly influencing factors. They are also, I might add, deceptive in the equating of ethnic differences.

Man, the archetype, is Eskimo, white man, Negro, or any other of the human races. Study the behavior of any timber wolf and you pretty well have comprehended and established the behavior pattern of this species generally. Study the behavior of white man without conventional deception and you have learned most of what concerns the basic nature of the Eskimo, the Indian, and Homo sapiens worldwide.

Temperamental differences in the Eskimo and Indian, apparently stemming from environment, are noticed on occasion. I attach no ethnic importance, however, to the fact that an Eskimo, for example, can wait out a three-day blizzard in a deeply reflective state, scarcely moving a muscle, while under these same conditions, most white men become petulant, and unless occupied in some utilitarian or other time-consuming way, suffer nervous repression. The prolonged Northern winter darkness could perhaps be the tempering influence of the Eskimo's life that enables him to bridge these gaps with a regulated passiveness.

Neither the Eskimo nor the Indian in his more natural environment has shown the apprehensions of the white man where long-time subsistence security is concerned. Something might be said here about white man's economic tension, caused largely through the fear of losing future, not immediate, economic security.

Eskimos, commonly believed to live under the most adverse climatic conditions, have been falsely said to lack a sense of humor. On the contrary, Eskimos laugh and show an extraordinary amount of gaiety and humor in their everyday life. Pretty much as all other races, they bridge many of their current problems by humorous banter.

On one occasion I had been out in the scrub forest of the Barrens photographing caribou at sub-zero temperatures. In operating the camera my right hand had been exposed so much it had puffed up considerably, not because of actual freezing but from reduced circulation through too prolonged exposure. While I was talking to an elderly Eskimo carver of ivory, he noticed my swollen hand—a condition very familiar to him. He, of course, saw the two mittens dangling at my side, and humorously asked if I had only one mitten. I proceeded to explain that operating the small mechanism of my camera called for too prolonged exposure of my right hand. "Yes," he said with a wry smile, "it is hard to pick lice with mittens on."

This is not a brand of humor apt to send an audience rolling in the aisles. It simply points out that the Eskimo, like the rest of us, enjoys the daily banter that goes with life's little problems everywhere, and meets much of his own adversity with an admirable sustaining levity.

It is difficult sometimes to know whether the Eskimo is being subtle or facetious. When he is hungry he reminds those about him that "somebody is hungry." There is no flaunting of the ego, no self-adulation, no personal accusations—"somebody has done something wrong" or "somebody is not very kind." How can anyone be disturbed by such impersonal though individualized blanket allusions? And what an insight, I might add, into the most difficult of human problems everywhere on earth—face-saving.

Eskimos in their early life and now when living apart from white man's diseases have been one of the most disease-free races in the world. Indeed, this should have great clinical value in appraising their living methods. If we cannot and do not, and perhaps never will, practice their methods, at least their early, original, natural health standard has proved far superior to our own.

When white men brought tuberculosis, smallpox, venereal diseases, and a host of other illnesses into the Eskimo villages, vast numbers of Eskimos were plagued and died. Living in close proximity with one another in their compact shelters, they were highly vulnerable to infection. The Canadian government has at long last been doing commendable work in stamping out tuberculosis and other diseases among Eskimos and Indians. They have for some time been flown out in large numbers to the various hospitals provided for them. Here, with new drug specifics for tuberculosis, combined with surgery and other treatment, cases of tuberculosis have been so reduced that facilities in these hospitals are now largely being used for other forms of disability among Eskimos and Indians, especially, for example, in the treatment of children's deformities.

At times when I am in the North, I am approached by press, radio, and TV for interview. A question often asked is, "What do you think we should do with the Eskimo and the Indian?" By the very nature of this question, I cannot resist asking in return, "What do you think the Eskimo and the Indian should do with us?" If this can be construed as a boomerang question, which it should be, perhaps we might gain some measure of decorum in placing ourselves in the Eskimo's or the Indian's position. White man has recklessly ravaged the natural resources upon which they depended and survived for ages. Indeed! What shall they do with the white man?!

The best answer I can suggest for: "What should we do with the Eskimo and the Indian?" with our responsibility and infinite debt to him, is, first ask the Eskimo and the Indian what he wants done; second, make some effort to reimburse him for the vast, reckless plunder of his resources which we have carried on, likely now at this perilous stage irreversible; finally, after getting his plan, help him to work toward his self-determining goal, not ours, respect his attitude and philosophy of life even though we cannot understand it, and quit meddling in his affairs beyond his rightful demand to have us fulfill our responsibility to him.

Villages of housing units with indoor plumbing are being built by the government for the Eskimo. These are small, mod-

The Eskimo and his art—the walrus hunter

ern units; but the outhouse properly constructed has proved to
be a much more sanitary unit than the present flush toilets
spilling sewage along the stratum of permafrost in hazardous
surface contamination, or dumping it into the nearest body of
water—too often also the main source of water supply.

A part of the Eskimo's livelihood in his housing communities
is gained from home industry, art carvings, and some outside
industrial employment. There seems to be a growing demand
for his home industry items, and this eventually may, in part,
provide an alternative to his white-man-despoiled natural
means of livelihood. Fortunately, through intelligent organization by the Department of Northern Affairs, the Eskimo no
longer has his works of art and craft filched from him by white
traders and individual tourists for a paltry sum. He now at last
has begun to demand a fair value for his work.

The younger Eskimo, of course, finds pleasure in the
gewgaws of modern industry, but the elders whom I have
interviewed over a half century have but one basic desire: they
want most of all their territorial domain and self-determina-
tion in a natural environment without interference.

In time it may be possible to provide villages of the Eskimo's
choosing and planning along the Northern coasts, where he
can carry on both arts and crafts for outside sale of his wares,
and which will also make possible his free run of the seas and
tundra for a share of naturalistic life. The success of such a
plan will depend on our ability to keep contaminating fallout
and industrial pollution out of his domain. We need to lend
him a monetary hand whenever we can, along with legislation
when he asks for it, not legislation imposed on him. Helping
him to restore his culture and encourage his naturalistic life is
a small recompense for our long and reckless incursion upon
his equity.

It is quite obvious that he will not be content with a day-in,
day-out industrial existence. He has shown in too many instances that he wants to wake in the morning and contemplate

the blue arctic sea with the calm, cultural, and natural outlook which is his heritage. If by his own choice his day becomes long and arduous, or short, reflective, and leisurely, this is what he should do, not what he would be required to do under the mandates of our own industrial habit.

Study of the Eskimo culture has dominated the interest of Northern explorers for a great many years. Eskimos by the very nature of their environment are perhaps the most unusual of all ethnic groups. Their life baffles us largely because we cannot understand their ability to carry on in a rigorous climate the naturalistic, happy, and viable existence which they have enjoyed.

We cannot insist that the Eskimo and Indian must be brought into our way of life. They look with grim suspicion on our ravaged forests, rivers transformed into open flowing sewers, lakes becoming cesspools, soil and air contaminated beyond reversible correction. They see plainly what most thoughtful men of science now consider as eventual industrial suicide.

A federal report on the Eskimo's problem gives the following: ". . . a hard look is being taken at results achieved so far, and a hard question asked: what exactly have we got, and what may we reasonably hope to get [from the Eskimo] for these massive expenditures?" The report goes on to say that for a government multimillion dollar outlay for the Eskimo, the return has been only one fifth this amount.

Here, on this premise, we have the Eskimo placed on a strictly monetary basis where the general public is griping because it cannot exact from him the last pound of flesh for the public budget.

The report indicates that ". . . it is too soon to say that these programs have failed—but they have certainly not succeeded."

Failed? They were cardinal failures and unwitting or intentional frauds upon the Eskimo's way of life at inception!

A scheme has been considered to blast an artificial harbor on the arctic coast with atomic energy, the so-called Project Chariot. If carried out, it will likely sound the death knell to arctic wildlife and to the Eskimo's culture and existence.

The Atomic Energy Commission wants to know by going ahead with the project, what effect fallout will have on life—"the nuclear effect on the biota." We do not have to go far for an answer to this proposed recklessness. Already the flesh of the caribou contains from 600 to 700 per cent more strontium 90 than the flesh of cattle in the rest of our country. Caribou feed on lichens. This is a rootless plant that attaches itself to rock and soil, deriving its nutriment from the dust in the air, driven down to earth by both summer and winter precipitation. It will readily be seen that fallout will get directly into these plants without having to be absorbed by the roots. Caribou living primarily on these lichens have already been placed in a perilous state from the fallout blown over great distances. There is here the potential of human and animal extinction. What will be the situation with these plants should fallout be rained directly down on the arctic prairie? The Eskimos, Indians, and whites will eat the remaining caribou, resulting in human deformities in tragically overwhelming numbers.

The report insists that the economic solution must be to "find something in the ground up there." Perhaps the first initial move in a basic plan should be to find something in our heads down here.

The task that lies before us where the Eskimo and the Indian are concerned, I believe, is to recognize that intelligence is an innate quality in them also, and no special prerogative of the white race. Nor is intelligence and a durable culture under any circumstance to be weighed primarily in terms of mechanization and industry. Anthropologists in recent years have made IQ tests of individuals living under what commonly we so glibly refer to as "savage" and "primitive" conditions—actually they are unencumbered natural conditions. In broad ethnic studies and recently in special experiments, though advantages of learning may not be immediately available, a high degree of intelligence is found among all naturalistic peoples over the world. During World War II, Japanese industrialists brought down to their factories some of the so-called "primitive" peoples, and rapidly trained them for work on assembly lines—in time finding prodigious mechanical and creative accomplishment among them. The experiments proved that the ability-spread between naturalistic routine processes and assembly-line operations was not nearly as great as believed. Many people will be surprised to know that most of the steel work in the building of New York skyscrapers is done by Indians.

Eskimos and Indians have always shown a remarkable capacity for learning and categorizing the elements and functions of their life in a natural environment. When I mentioned to them that it is strange no written language was used early in their culture, they told me that in a naturalistic life there was little need for it, and that "it is better to have knowledge in our heads than in books."

While books are, of course, infinitely important in our communication of knowledge and necessary documents in keeping the record of man's progress, assimilating knowledge instead of filing it in a library has become a highly important factor in our recent rather explosive examination of "What's wrong with our educational system?" The academic student is apt to get little of what he has perused in books unless he thoroughly assimilates it and carries the final result in his head to make it not referentially usable but spontaneously functional. Most of what the college student acquires comes from lectures, the oral method of teaching used by naturalistic man down through the ages. Compared to naturalistic man, how much do most of our students, we might ask, learn directly from natural phenomena without academic aid?

Also, let us not overlook that not so long ago, only a few of our own white population could read or write. The comparison should have been made at the early period of general illiteracy. Most races, including the Eskimo and Indian, now have literacy. At this time, there are more Eskimos and Indians speaking both their native language and English than whites speaking their own language and the Eskimo and Indian tongues.

Recently, I examined the Cree-English dictionary, compiled by the Anglican Church. I found a Cree vocabularly vastly beyond the education of our average city dweller. The Cree have terms in their language for common applications of daily life as well as for understanding and categorizing the natural environmental phenomena. For example, he will say: "Kichichimao" ("He starts from the shore in a canoe"), "Muskisinikao" ("She is making moccasins"), "Kimewun" ("It rains"), "Kimewunisew" ("He is out in the rain"), "Kimewuniskakoo" ("It rains upon him"). Thus, we are made aware of the term's meaning by the very picture it conjures.

When new devices and mechanical innovations along with white man's ways were introduced, natives were quick to coin their own nomenclature and descriptive expressions for these devices. The airplane, now a part of his life, is "pimiyakun" ("that which flies"). Most often their terms are far more descriptive and delineating than our own. Take our coffee for example; by the Indian it is called "mukuta muskikewapoo." Translated, it means "black medicine water." Can you beat it in both descriptive and connotative brilliance?

We might earnestly consider the fact that the so-called primitive peoples have lived a naturalistic, rich life for thousands of years without the problems now threatening our existence. Can we in our modern processes hope to live out many more decades without succumbing to the devastation of our whole natural world? On this premise I suggest we might ponder the age-old wisdom of the incredible naturalistic man.

8

RETROSPECTION

SOME weeks ago I stood upon the winter shores of Hudson Bay, fascinated by the vastness and rugged beauty of the up-turned pack ice caught in the vermilion glow of the setting sun. The end of ice was lost in a nebulous horizon. While observing this vast frozen sea, I was forced to conclude rather immodestly that my years of application to the wilderness left me with a visual advantage over that of the casual tourist when contemplating such a natural spectacle. Ability to see is certainly not a simple visual function. We need, I think, a long, cultivated awareness to register the fullest impressions.

The common saying that men climb mountains because the mountains are there can only be a trite subterfuge in the effort to capture the elusive, real reason why some irresistibly scale heights. On no stronger premise am I able to qualify the fascination which the winter wilderness has held for me.

Days of variable uncertainties, tussles with rough weather,

"... the vastness and rugged beauty of the upturned pack ice .

elements of danger, hunger, and, perhaps worst of all, a seeming frustration after best effort—these at times, one would, if
they could be anticipated, avoid by every commanding resource. Yet, the overall problems now seem to have been as
integral a part of and as essential to life's fulfillment as the
happy events. Life without strife could lose its inherent purpose and interest.

We have seen in reading significant biographies that no life
can have real meaning that does not show a few consequent
scars. As the caribou herd without the wolf pack on its migra-
tory heels becomes less vigorous, so is man apt to fall short of
full maturity without a substantial share of adversity.

Any reflection upon past life will inevitably point up a
change in our present way of life. This morning I shopped in a
supermarket, checking out a little more than twenty dollars'
worth of provisions. These were carried to my car in paper

bags in the arms of a service boy and placed beside me in the seat. Back near the beginning of the century I prepared to spend a winter in the wilderness with about a twenty- to thirty-dollar grubstake. A hundred pounds of flour in those earlier days cost ninety-eight cents and had vast potentials for a variety of exciting foods. The flour was bought in fifty-pound-size cloth bags for convenience in packing on the trail. When the fifty pounds had been used up, the bag was opened at the seams, washed, and became important as a dish towel. If one could remember on which end of the flour bag to disengage the stitching cords, ripping the seam was comparable in effect to opening a modern zipper. A slab of lean, high-grade, sugar-cured bacon, weighing about seven pounds, cost not seventy cents per pound but seventy cents for the entire slab—or about ten cents per pound. Hams were comparably priced. Potatoes were fifty cents for a hundred-pound sack in any farmer's field. Sometimes I exchanged a few freshly caught fish for a sack of potatoes. Sun-dried apricots, apples, pears, peaches, prunes, or raisins cost ninety-eight cents per twenty-pound wood caddy. These supplied vitamin C. If you had a root cellar where fresh apples could be kept from freezing, a barrel of apples, including the wooden barrel, cost one dollar and fifty cents. Twenty pounds of sugar cost less than a dollar and a ten-pound pail of pancake syrup about fifty cents. Salt in a cloth sack, containing five pounds, cost a nickel. The empty sack had several practical uses. Coffee, tea, rice, baking powder, etc., were in proportionate value. Add up the provision equivalent of from twenty to thirty dollars in the bulk items named, and you will have some estimate of comparable costs then and now, and how easy it was to winter in a wilderness cabin on thirty dollars or less.

For me early in life the handwriting was clearly on the wall: "Garner a wilderness grubstake and you garner leisure." I equated dollar value with leisure time value. In short, how much leisure time will a dollar buy?

Autumn was the seasonal doorway that opened on a winter

of leisure and adventure in the wilderness. Now there would be no insects or summer heat. Winter employment in the city was always at a short ebb in those earlier days. Let someone else step into the industrial void, if any, that I might be leaving.

Waiting in a chicken-wire kennel at the city limits were four sled dogs—Mackenzie River malamutes that had come down from the upper Mackenzie River the previous year as little puppies, mere handfuls, in a small basket—now sufficiently grown to begin their three months' training for the winter's sled harness. A Peterborough, Prospector Model, all-cedar canoe was stored in the loft of a barn, where the four sled dogs were kenneled.

Every evening after work I would refine and fondle my camping equipment. The very feel of it had a magic touch. With the famous mined Arkansas oilstones, I honed ax and knife to razor sharpness—the ax handle itself rubbed to a natural wood finish with an oil compound until it was a wood lover's delight. The Winchester .30-30 carbine was taken from its moosehide case at every opportunity and sighted at an imaginary creature—the street corner gas lamp—for a simulated shot. The gunstock was hand rubbed again and again to a satiny rich grain luster, the gun then routinely returned to its case. Envious droppers-in to see the equipment would argue muzzle velocity, trajectory, bullet expansion, and the relative weights and killing power of bullets—a special language that only a few of us could understand. My never-failing winter meat supply annually shot in the wilderness disproved many of the opposing ballistic arguments leveled by my visitors at the traditional .30-30 carbine standby. The .22 pistol was the complement gun for small game.

In those years guns were an important essential in the winter program. (Today in Canada, guns, except the .22 caliber rifle, are outlawed except in hunting season.) On first reaching the wilderness, partridge or ptarmigan, rabbits (snowshoe and arctic hares), and even ducks, shot with the .22 pistol, balanced up the store supply of food—along with fish. Once the deep freeze of early winter was well on, a moose, caribou or deer was shot and hung in an elevated cache—a small shed mounted on stilts, reached only by a removable ladder.

Meat, of course, is the most costly item anywhere in figuring food budgets from commercial markets. Normally, and without cost, this was well supplied in the wilderness. With four dogs to feed, a great deal depended on the rifle and the fishnet. (Nets now are outlawed except for commercial fishermen.) A quantity of whitefish was netted in the fall and dried for the dogs, although some net fishing was done under the ice.

Hundred-pound sacks of finely ground chick feed or mixed grain meal were added to the provision load for dog food. Such cereal, cooked and combined with whitefish, fat, rough meat and entrails from wilderness-killed animals, kept the dogs in fine condition. Sometimes I ate some of the dogs' cereal, cooked alone as breakfast food and mixed with reconstituted dry whole milk. Some of it I had ground to Indian meal, and after cooking and cooling it as a porridge, I mixed it with the sourdough pancake batter.

The day of departure from the city toward the wilderness was always, no matter how often repeated, one of special excitement. The sled dogs, when released from their chicken-wire enclosures, went into a joyous frenzy. They did not, of course, understand the impending rail or steamship transportation ordeal, and when I had to muzzle them and place them on chain leashes in the baggage car of a train or in the hold of a ship, sometimes by regulation in crates, they seemed to impart a demeanor of certain doom. I went to them frequently to soothe their "hung-dog" feelings. They wagged their tails, moaned anxiously. Now and then, they let out a restrained but long-drawn-out howl revealing their part-wolf breed, usually bringing an amused and abiding smile from the baggage agent in charge.

Passengers were always intensely curious. Also, you could depend on the press to show up whenever they were made aware of the northward course of sled dogs and driver. I tried to act casual about my undertaking, but inwardly during these youthful years I was more than enjoying the crowd's interest and press notices. Transfer of the dogs from the railhead to some ship heading into the North created a wilderness atmosphere for tourists and other boat passengers, who now as a result of seeing sled dogs, Indians, outpost sites, etc., were getting the flavor of adventure they earnestly had hoped would round out their excursion. They were especially intrigued when they saw snowshoes, dog sled, and other winter gear. To most of the ship's passengers, the prospect of living in a winter wilderness was awesome to contemplate. If they had read the fictional fancies of James Oliver Kerwood, they saw the prospect with a kind of romantic terror.

Boats traveling into the North along ocean coasts, Hudson and James Bays, Lake Winnipeg, the Yukon River, the Great Lakes, and other such waters, have been very generous and accommodating in letting off wilderness-bound trippers, prospectors, surveyors, and various other wilderness travelers at other than regular stops. On coastal trips the task of getting to shore from steamboats when the seas were running high provided a most dramatic sight for the passengers. Whenever the boat could pull in behind a headland near a river's mouth for a calmer sea, this was the procedure followed for reaching the river embarkation point by canoe. The loaded canoe could then be lowered into the water by crane, a nearby camp pitched in the lee of the headland until calmer water allowed canoe travel along the coastal strip into the river's mouth.

In such ship-to-shore embarkation, I would have too much of a load in the canoe for the sled dogs to ride. After the dogs had been unmuzzled and freed from their tethers or crates aboard ship, I would start out for shore with the heavily laden canoe. For a moment the dogs would stand contemplating their plight, then leap into the water and swim toward me. This entire episode became drama and romance for the passengers. Kodaks and the famous dollar box cameras by the dozen snapped along the ship's rail. Reaching shore, my four sled dogs would systematically and with perfect coordination give me a shower bath as they shook themselves dry.

My meeting on the shore with the dogs was a special occasion. For the first time in their lives, the dogs enjoyed their full freedom from leashes, crates and chicken-wire kennels. Freedom for both man and beast is undoubtedly the most precious of all life's attributes. The dogs, now ashore, rolled in the forest humus, sniffed out every cranny where there was a strange odor, ranged and whooped it up generally. I felt their mood. I, too, on this shore had cut bonds, conventional and industrial. While the dogs were making their adjustment, I stood and watched the last ship of the season and the friends I had made aboard disappear around the headland. I was reminded of the remark made by a former wilderness companion of mine, "Now, dammit, at last we can holler for help and not be heard."

Retrospection as considered here does not imply that the wilderness is gone and is to be regarded only in the past tense. Vast areas remain to challenge the most avid wilderness enthusiast. While dog sleds are rapidly leaving the scene, many are still in use in forest and along the arctic coasts. The jeep, as we have seen, did not entirely replace the saddle horse, nor is it likely to do so; and where the motorized toboggan is concerned, the harness dog will, no doubt, be held over with as much tradition and affection.

It would be false, of course, to suggest that one does not retrospectively suffer a certain nostalgia for the early wilderness. While we accept the transportation conveniences and adventure bypasses of a modern age, there continues an inescapable awareness that a certain degree of rugged and elemental living was, could be, and still is desirable. I have in a

". . . a certain degree of rugged and elemental living . . . is desirable."

previous chapter hinted at a kind of favorable regard for crisis or the hazards of adventure. Were all of life to be regulated on a noncritical and comfortable basis, it could become easy to the point of monotony. The news reporter who returned from years of covering the battlefront only to find normal life as he had previously known it purposeless and journalistically void by comparison, was not wholly rational in his failure to readjust, but I can understand in a sense how he felt. The late Stewart Edward White, outdoor writer and adventurer, on one of his packhorse trips found the going so uniform and uneventful days on end, he was thankful for the critical moment when

Nellie, a rather awkward pack animal, would stumble and fall again in some precarious part of the trail.

While conveniences and luxuries can be encouraging and delightful attributes, continued proliferation of convenience and mechanization could sweep out of existence our most cherished individualistic and naturalistic values. If, for example, I have preferred to drive a dog team or pull a toboggan manually over hundreds of miles of inspiring wilderness rather than always be picked up by a plane with ski landing gear and whisked over the same route in a few hours, it isn't that I fail to understand the expedience of the fast transportation I now occasionally use. It is merely that when I am packed in a metal tube and hurled through space, I lose all contact with the natural values in the area I seek to enjoy. A man who had seen the Central Patricia region twice by air only said, "I've covered every inch of that ground." It will be apparent what his reaction was when an attempt was made to discuss various features and aspects which I had seen in fifty years of periodical travel in the area by canoe and dog team.

If I want a picture painted manually with brushes by an imaginative artist in the serenity of the wilderness or countryside, rather than by a computer-controlled painting machine, as someone suggested recently that art will come to, it is because the artist's efforts seem to hold out a better chance for me to retain my sanity and what seems to me life's greatest and most profoundly satisfying values. What is more, I don't want books conceived and written by computers either, while there are still aspiring scribes around to do it—and that includes me.

Though there be a gutter, man does not have to lie like a drunk in it. If retrospection has taught me anything, it is that we *can* choose what we want. We *can* exclude gadgetry. We *can* prefer walking to riding, and in many instances, perhaps, reach our destination—pleasure—much sooner. Travel in the wilderness with a hand-drawn toboggan or by dog sled may be just as significant and rewarding today as it was a few decades ago. We need only the wisdom to discriminate.

Those born within the copyright date of this book are likely still to have a wilderness to enjoy, and if their voyages are in winter, that wilderness will be ever wilder, more remote, more entrancing. Dorothy Wordsworth in October 1802 wrote in her journal, "It is a pleasure to the real lover of Nature to give winter all the glory he can, for summer will make its own way, and speak its own praises."

9

THE MAGIC EFFECT
OF WINTER CLOTHES

MAN's wide range of adjustment to temperature extremes over the earth has made clothes one of the most significant factors in his entire exploration and habitation progress.

If man originated as tropical animal (a moot question), the discovery of clothes must have provided his first means of departure from the tropical zone. Whether he experimented with plant fibers for low-temperature clothing before he sought to "borrow" the coats of furbearing animals, we are unable to say. The finding of numerous flint skin scrapers, as well as arrow- and spearheads, appears to indicate that as man ate the flesh of animals, he began to see the merit of using the animal's body skin as covering for himself. Sometime along his evolution he learned by necessity to cure and eventually tan these skins. If, however, the Eskimo's forebears descended from those who made this tropical departure, the Eskimo is certainly a far-ranging anomaly.

During the arctic midsummer, mosquitoes breed on the tundra by the insufferable billions. The early Eskimo did not

fare too well against them in the summer heat with his animal-
skin clothing. When cloth clothing was introduced into the
Eskimo's life, he gained a marked degree of protection from
insects, and comfort in the summer heat.

During the winter, on the other hand, the Eskimo has apparently always been more than master over his own situation.
He kills the caribou in August for winter garments, when the
fur is most adaptable to clothing, using one suit of young or,
when available, unborn, very soft fur next to his body from
spring-killed animals, another suit of adult caribou fur outward. Mukluks—his standard footwear—are generally of seal.
He uses hair seal for the tops, which reach just under the
knees, and heavier ugrug or square flipper seal for the soles.
Caribou and moose, soft-tanned, on the other hand, are used
for the low, dry temperatures.

Eskimo women manage an ingenious, rolled, waterproof
seam in seal boots, a technique astounding to anyone seeing
the boots for the first time. Since the tanning of sealskins only
partially keeps the mukluks waterproof, they have to be
changed about every three days and dried in the interval during the mild season to prevent bacterial decomposition of the
hide. Eskimos in close contact with commercial trading centers, of course, use all manner of factory-made footwear and
clothing items. Yard goods from trading posts are their primary clothing purchases, since they prefer their own styles and
craftsmanship, thereby avoiding the high cost of factory-made
garments.

For centuries the most plausible solution to the clothes problem for the white man on his winter exploration of the arctic
was to adopt the Eskimo's dress in its entirety. Eskimo garments are so ingeniously patterned that they avoid all possible
restriction of limbs during physical activity. Down through the
years Eskimos have surpassed the white man in developing
such free-action clothing.

We had an excellent example of this skill when garments, using Eskimo patterns, were being made commercially from pile for military service. Copying Eskimo patterns proved to be not as simple as first presumed. The Eskimo garments which were dismantled for individual pattern pieces did not, to the surprise of commercial clothing designers, shape up in their hands like the original Eskimo garments that offered such remarkable freedom of body movement. A very ingenious shirring and joining in the assembly of rather complex pattern pieces by the Eskimo women proved that their garments were made with extraordinary knowledge of functional design and skill—no doubt of longtime development. Commercial firms, failing utterly to simulate the Eskimo patterns on the first attempt, had additional Eskimo garments flown down from the arctic for more careful study of the patterns, so that proper integration of pattern parts could take place. The construction was found to be quite involved. When finally the wearer's limbs could move freely through their maximum functional positions without the least restriction, the imitating of Eskimo techniques finally was in part resolved.

Fur still has an important place in the making of cold-weather garments, but quilted down seems to have, in recent years and in larger measure, displaced fur both in practicability and cost. The chief reason is that down garments "breathe" more freely; that is, they allow air to move more readily to and from the body to reduce condensation, while the garments at the same time maintain their high insulating value. Down has great facility for trapping the innumerable dead-air spaces which form the basic insulation principle.

In my own research of down garments, I have found that considerable "breathing" value is lost in some garments by the exclusive use of synthetic fibers in place of cotton for encasing the down. The reason for this lies in the nonporous nature of synthetic fibers, which allows air to pass only between the warp and woof of the weave. In cotton, air movement passes not only between the woven threads but through them as well. In selecting down garments, therefore, make sure that the encasing fabrics are cotton or a combination of cotton and synthetic yarns. These combination materials have the advantage of increased strength with some loss of porousness, though they are a needed compromise in rugged travel where strength is important.

The insulating miracle of goose and duck down is an interesting one to consider. The down from the eider duck is perhaps the most extraordinary in this respect, but its scarcity and consequent high cost makes it unavailable for most general use. Northern domestic goose down has a high insulating quality. Down from the Northern white domestic goose—a longtime descendant of the snow goose—ranks highest of the goose downs, but the darker shades also rank high.

Pile (a furlike material having a cloth instead of a natural skin base) is quite satisfactory for winter garments, providing it is a high-grade, double-faced, full-furred, soft pile such as that used by the military forces, especially when it is used in complement with a slipover anorak (windbreaker) made from thin, high-count material of cotton or a combination of cotton and nylon. The common piles used in commercial street clothing are usually a thinly furred, short-hair or synthetic fiber, a single-surface material not suited for winter wilderness clothing. They serve quite well for linings in conventional street clothes where a light pile is required.

An outstanding quality of the single- and double-faced, full-furred pile is its high "breather" (ventilating) property. Since the base of pile to which the fur is bonded is porous cloth instead of animal skin as in fur pelts, there is free movement of moist air to and from the body, thus cutting down on condensation. A fur pelt "worn" by an animal is a complex, living, highly functional organ and has a great deal more efficiency and adaptation to varying temperatures and other conditions of weather than when tanned and worn as a dead covering over the human body. Some explorers have preferred pile garments to fur because of their greater ventilating quality. The Eskimo with his long and varied experience with fur was quick to grasp the value of top-grade pile. Some Eskimo women have used it in combination with fur in their garments in such a way that it can scarcely be distinguished from fur.

When a double-faced pile parka, for example, is worn with a thin anorak over it, two air-space insulating layers are created—between the cloth base and one's body, and between the cloth base and the anorak—with, of course, the thousands of dead-air spaces between the fur fibers and in the fur fibers themselves. The anorak thus provides the pile with an insulating value comparable to quilting. A functional advantage on the trail when using the anorak over pile is that the anorak can be peeled off as activity begins to supply warmth—expediting the gradual clothes reduction process described in Chapter 10.

We get a very good idea of the basic insulation principles involved in a parka-anorak combination when we cover ourselves with an ordinary wool blanket. Since wool fibers are hollow, and the wool when fluffed into a nap creates additional air spaces, we get fair insulating value from the wool blanket alone. But if we cover the wool blanket with a very thin, yet porous, high-count complement material on both sides of the blanket, or at least on the outside, at once we discover a remarkable increase in the warmth of the blanket, far in excess of the total insulating value of the separate items. With the thin material covering we have trapped, still further, innumerable insulating air spaces in the nap between the blanket weave and the cotton covering. A rabbit-skin robe, as I pointed out in Chapter 2, becomes much warmer if it is quilted between sheets of thin, high-count material. We experience the same insulating principle in the making of a bed quilt—two thin coverings trapping myriad air spaces in the bat of wool or down. An ordinary sweater, for example, becomes much warmer if worn under a thin cotton outer shirt rather than over it.

Down, in order to be used at all, must, needless to say, be quilted between thin, high-count materials, although tanned loon skins with the down still attached to the skin have been used by Eskimos for parkas.

If you have watched birds settling down on a perch in extremely cold weather you will see them ruffle their down until it fluffs out almost twice the normal body-covering depth. As has been proved by laboratory tests, the fluffing increases warmth, since the fluff provides additional thickness and dead-air spaces.

Most down garments, therefore, are quilted loosely enough to keep the down in fairly full fluff. Some objection has been raised concerning the bulkiness of down garments, but this bulkiness somehow does not impede the free movement of arms and legs as much as stiffer, less bulky materials do, because of the softness, flexibility, and light weight of down and the generally very thin quilting material used in making up these garments.

Some down garments have an additional draping material stitched lightly to the outside of the quilted lining as a facing to dress up the garment for more conventional appearance, used principally to hide the biscuitlike surface of the quilting. This facing has the value of creating additional air spaces in the sewed depressions between the quilted bulges and outer covering, again appreciably improving the warmth of the garment. For wilderness garments it is better for convertible advantages to have this outer covering removable.

If now, in selecting our full garb, we start our general list of clothing next to the body, may I suggest that woolen underwear be chosen. There are various kinds of cold-weather underwear recommended by manufacturer and user which are not wool. Some are wool with a cotton or synthetic fiber facing next to the skin. The so-called "thermal" underwear is generally of cotton, containing multiple dead-air-space construction. None will have the actual warmth and the warm feeling of wool against the body when the clamminess from perspiration occurs. The only test for trail underwear is long, energetic exercise under sub-zero conditions, and wool is best under these conditions. Cotton "thermal" type underwear, while satisfactory for conventional, normal use, gets one into trouble on the trail at very low temperatures. If the manufacturers would use the "thermal" principle with wool yarns, retaining the multiple dead-air spaces, much would be gained. The rib and other weaves even in common wool underwear do provide to a low degree the multiple air space principle. If wool underwear against your body is not for you after a fair and comprehensive trial (don't give up at the onset), then try part wool, or wool with an inner-woven facing of cotton or synthetic yarn materials, with some loss, of course, in the warm feeling of all wool.

Wool underwear can usually be tolerated by almost everybody after being worn a short time on the trail, since the initial "itch" soon leaves. Even when damp with perspiration, wool, unlike cotton, does not feel clammy. As I indicated in Chapter 2, it is important that woolen underwear be donned in a room considerably below room-comfort temperatures, to avoid that first indoor "shower" of perspiration. Synthetic fiber underwear does dry faster than others, which is a valuable factor on the winter trail where drying is a problem, but it does not measure up to wool in warmth and a feeling of continued comfort following perspiration in low temperatures. In order of rank, choose: all wool, wool combination, synthetic fiber, and last—cotton thermal type. See Chapter 10 for a description of fur underwear.

Down-garment manufacturers make a quilted down undergarment that is usually worn over the next-to-the-body under-

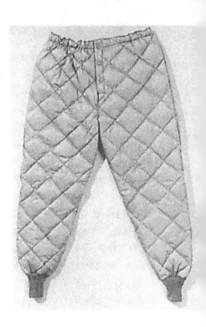

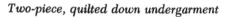
Two-piece, quilted down undergarment

wear. The down garments come in two-piece style, shirt and drawers. These are excellent garments when a thin, high-count material windbreaker is worn over the down shirt, and a pair of thin, flexible, high-count-material duck pants are also worn over the down drawers. The combination gives a delightful feeling of ease and lightness with remarkable warmth. Some down shirts are designed on the Eskimo artigi pattern; that is, the back portion dips down like a broad tail in cut to cover a part of the seat—eliminating that cold spot at the lower part of the back at the juncture of shirt and trousers which is created when bending at the waist. Also, it forms an insulated pad to sit on.

A desirable combination in part for cold-weather dress is light wool underwear next to the body, fishnet underwear over this, followed by the down undergarments—the light, high-count-material duck pants and a windbreaker. Seldom when active is it necessary to don the outside parka, except, of course, on mug-ups or other stops. The so-called fishnet un-

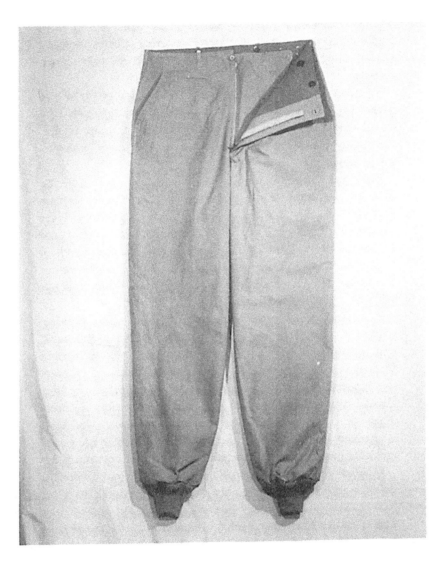

Light, high-count-material duck pants

derwear resembles the material used for minnow nets. When this net underwear is put on between garments, the mesh in combination with inner and outer covering creates dead-air spaces, supplying an excellent body "breather" type of insulation.

Whether or not one is attracted to the wearing of fur or pile parkas in preference to down, I have found that most men who travel wilderness trails, regardless of outside garment choice, are highly pleased with the addition of the down undergarments described.

Some quilted garments are made with extruded synthetic fiber fillers instead of down. Others have processed feathers and various other inexpensive fillers, even cotton bats. Their insulating qualities fall far below the goose down, and should be chosen only in dire need as an economy measure; and, of course, used only under those conditions that are well within the temperature limits of their insulating value. Where budgets will allow, the choice is obvious.

Fur parkas have been made from various pelts: caribou, white fox, wolf, lynx, and others. They are warm, picturesque, and expensive. A popular parka used in the Far North is made from Hudson's Bay Company duffel cloth—a heavy, blanket-like material. These duffel parkas have a complementary blue outside windbreaker covering of cotton or nylon material. Then, of course, we have the parkas made from pile, both single and double. Pile is also a satisfactory liner for outer-covering materials, such as duffel or high-count cotton fabrics.

Quilted goose down parkas or those made with a flexible double-faced pile used in combination with a windbreaker are the most easily available and most practical choice. The United States Army has over the years used parkas made from both single and double pile, in combination with a separate windbreaker or anorak over the pile unit. Both are of the pullover type. These have been in surplus at attractive prices. Their short length is a drawback, and should have a pile extension added to reach just above the knees.

The author in pile and fur parka, with wolverine fur ruff.
Mittens are of Indian-tanned moosehide and white wolf fur.
Note sandal-type snowshoe harness.

Quilted down parka with wolverine ruff

All parkas need a ruff of wolverine or wolf around the hood opening. Some ruffs are made with a combination of these two furs. There is a common, mistaken belief that frost rime does not adhere to wolverine fur. Frost rime does adhere, but less so than to most other furs, and the rime can be beaten off more readily.

Most commercial parkas come with zipper closures. These zippers are sometimes complemented with a buttoned-over or Velcro sealing flap. Velcro is a tape with a burr surfacing, patterned somewhat after the stickers or burrs that inadvertently fasten themselves to you as you pass through a weedy field. You press the two tapes together to fasten the garment, and merely pull the tapes apart to open it. The opening process sounds as though you were tearing cloth, but with repeated use no apparent harm is done and the Velcro seems to maintain its bond indefinitely.

The front-opening parka is convenient because it can be opened like a coat when needed along the trail to prevent perspiration, and is more easily removed or donned. But I have found that the parka which must be pulled over the head like a sweater, though less convenient to don and remove, is a warmer, simpler garment, and much less of a nuisance where obstinate zippers and buttons must be handled in sub-zero temperatures. Also, the front remains softer and more flexible without the doubled button or zipper-facing material and metal zipper mechanism. A constant butting of the knees against the stiffening construction of zipper mechanism on open-front garments is somewhat distressing over a long trail and causes additional fatigue. If the pullover type of parka is desired, it can be custom-made. Or, the standard garment can be altered by removing the entire zipper mechanism, buttons, Velcro fasteners, double facing, etc., and sewing the front together. To overcome the stiffness at the front, one manufacturer has made its parkas with the opening off to one side, which helps to a limited degree, but the parka still does not have the full flexibility of the pullover type.

A windbreaker, sometimes called an anorak, of very thin, high-count material, knee length, with parka hood, having a fur ruff of wolverine or wolf, is one of the most valuable items of clothing in any season. The garment weighs but ounces and is used alternatively with the main parka while the wearer is very active and less protection is needed. The ruff on the windbreaker should be supplied with nylon cord loops. These serve as buttonholes for fastening the ruff onto buttons which have been sewn to the windbreaker hood. The ruff can then be removed so that the windbreaker can be used in any season.

A complementary outside garment to the parka is the short pants. They can be made of quilted down, pile, or fur. Short pants are simply a pair of loose-fitting pants that come to the knees, made large enough to slip readily over the regular pants. (See Chapter 10 for their variable uses.) They were

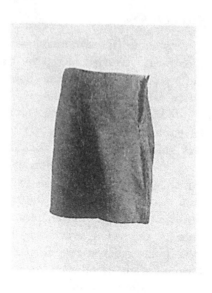

The short pants—a complementary outside garment

developed during the high period of arctic exploration to pro-
tect the femoral arteries, which come close to the surface on
the inside of the upper legs. Legs need additional insulation
here if the arterial bloodstreams are not to be chilled and rob
the lower legs and feet of warmth. In fact, arteries that come
close to the surface, unless well insulated against the cold, tend
to chill the entire body. Short pants have been worn by some
early explorers under other trousers. I found this inconvenient
because the short pants when worn underneath cannot readily
be donned and removed at the required intervals. I made mine
to fit over outside trousers, so that I could slip these short pants
on and off at varying times, simultaneously with the donning
or removing of the parka during stops. Eskimos have most
often made these short pants from polar bear skins and have
worn them over other pants.

Mittens are made from a variety of materials: fur, quilted
down, pile, Indian-tanned buckskin, moosehide, and Indian- or
Eskimo-tanned caribou hides. Whatever is used, the highly

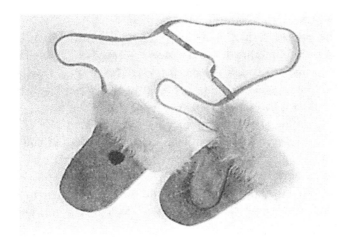

Moosehide mittens suspended on a thong

important factors are that the hands must be as functional as possible with the mittens on. The mittens must, therefore, be so constructed that one's hands can be individually withdrawn and reinserted without having to draw the mitten of one hand on or off with the other. Mittens need a flare opening for this. The flare opening does not mean a long, funnel-like gauntlet in the usual sense, but rather a short flare—just enough to create a ready opening. Such mittens are then suspended on a cord or thong around the neck, at a level that provides convenient, quick, periodical withdrawal and reinsertion of the hands. (See illustration.) The thong around the neck is an important addition. A mitten could otherwise be lost in the snow under varying circumstances of activity. To dig up a half acre of snow or the backtrail with one hand exposed at 40 below, looking for a mitten, obviously poses a hazard. Also, at times when travel is rugged, the hands may have to be bared, off and on, to prevent perspiration. When off, the mittens should then dangle at one's side. Hands also need to be bared at times for various purposes, such as adjusting snowshoe harness, operating a camera, unbuttoning garments, etc.

The mittens I find most satisfactory are made from soft, porous, Indian-tanned moose, deer, or caribou hide. These have a liner inserted, made from Hudson's Bay Company duffel, that reaches to the top of the mitten flare; and inside the duffel liner a pair of wristlets that reach to the knuckles.

A question may arise as to how snow is kept out of the flared mitten. This is no problem, because the knitted cuffs on a parka fit into the mitten somewhat like the tapered cork in a bottle, sealing out the possibility of snow getting in. Also, parka sleeves with knit cuffs should be long enough to bag slightly, the baggy sleeve-ends then closing over the mitten opening.

The above-mentioned wristlets of the army pattern, available in army surplus stores, should be used to complement the mittens. They come down over the palm of the hand, allowing only exposure of the fingers. Such wristlets, exposing only the fingers, allow the hands to be removed from the mittens for longer periods when operating a camera, firing a gun, adjusting snowshoe lashings, unbuttoning garments, etc., because the ulna and radial arteries that lie close to the surface at the wrists are well protected against the cold, giving much the same insulating effect as that just described in covering the femoral arteries with short pants.

Fur can be used for the backs of mittens if desired for additional warmth and a note of wilderness-garb flavor, but it should not be fur with too thick a hide that will rob the mitten of its important flexibility. August-killed caribou, lynx, wolf, or fox is suitable. Pile or quilted down, being very flexible, will serve for this mitten-backing as well as fur. I have found, however, that if one can get a soft, Indian-tanned, highly porous moosehide for making the mittens, and if one adds the duffel liner and the fur-trimmed wristlets, this combination is adequate, less bulky, and more adaptive to trail functions than fur. Fur mittens with commercially tanned leather palms are generally poor. The leather is a rapid conductor of heat from the hands.

Down mittens are also very satisfactory—preferably if made with a soft Indian- or Eskimo-tanned moosehide, caribou, or deerskin palm, not leather. The blotterlike porousness of these native-tanned hides, with their thousands of tiny dead-air spaces, makes them warm, flexible, and strong material for mittens. One manufacturer has provided a double section for the hands in its down mittens. The purpose is to allow closer contact with the leather palm, making the mitten more functional when working with mountain-climbing equipment, with an ax, or other field items. To gain more insulation for the palm of one's hand when not using equipment, and to regain warm hands, the hands are slipped out of the front section of the mitten into the other section, which is also quilted with down on the palm side. The idea can, of course, be adapted to mittens of any material. Again, however, a warning—avoid constriction of hand freedom in the bulk.

Footwear has probably created more problems than any other aspect of winter garb. Military services have struggled long and diligently for a possible solution. We can best approach this problem by considering winter footwear in two indispensable, complementary categories: waterproof footwear for days of thaw and around camp where campfires can create a similar wet condition; and extreme cold-, dry-weather footwear of a highly porous type when no moisture is encountered except overflow on ice under snow. Extremely low temperatures produce desert-like dryness.

The temperature distinction between these wet and dry conditions is not always sharply defined. It is possible, for example, to use waterproof footwear down to zero and even below without discomfort, although this varies considerably with each individual. Some people seem to have better circulation of blood in their extremities than others.

The duffel sock

In considering cold-weather clothes items, it must be borne in mind that all waterproof materials essentially have poor insulating value, for they are rapid conductors of heat from the body. Soft, porous materials that are poor conductors of heat but good insulators, on the other hand, are not waterproof, and are warm only when kept dry.

Efforts have been made in the construction of footwear to sandwich porous materials between sheets of rubber to gain both waterproofing and insulating value. However, this results in serious condensation, and leads to an unsatisfactory item of footwear. Commercial-leather boots are wholly unsuitable for cold-weather footwear.

The practical solution on a winter wilderness journey, therefore, is to include two basic kinds of footwear: waterproof and

Indian-tanned moosehide moccasin and duffel sock

extreme cold-weather types. The most practical commercial waterproof kind I have found is the lightweight, four- or five-buckle overshoe fitted to stockinged feet, *not to shoes*. (Avoid the heavy-weight, laborer's overshoe.) Heavy-weight wool knit socks, over which a single pair of duffel socks, felted Finn socks, or similar types is worn, provide the insulating liner for such overshoes. Most duffel socks reach just above the ankle, the knitted socks reaching under the knees. Because overshoes are moulded with a depression to fit the heel of a shoe, it becomes necessary to cement about two average felt lifts into the heel void. With a little use the lifts give the stockinged foot good contour bearing. Overshoes selected to fit over socks rather than over shoes become significantly smaller in size, usually two sizes smaller. This size reduction, along with the choice of lightweight overshoes, gives a moccasinlike feeling to the step. (Do not attempt to use zipper-type overshoes. With rough use the zippers will jam hopelessly.)

Winter trousers need knitted cuffs that can be inserted into the top of the overshoe. The trouser legs then bag slightly over the overshoe, sealing out snow. The overshoe is far superior to the common laced rubber pacs, made with leather tops and rubber bottoms, quite popular with hunters. These are perspiration generators.

For cold, dry weather, the so-called mukluk, popular in the arctic, is a style of footwear that fits over the trouser leg and reaches to just under the knee. Most mukluks have a draw-cord or thong around the top to seal out snow. The thong should be tied loosely to avoid impairing circulation in the legs, which might risk freezing the feet. Moccasins, more popular in the forest area, are largely of a type reaching about six inches above the ankle. They can be worn over the knitted trouser cuff, or under it, as desired. Where the trousers are used without the knitted cuff, as some prefer, the moccasin is laced snug, but not tight, to the stockinged leg, the trousers then worn loose over the moccasin.

A popular mukluk in the Far North for cold, dry weather is one made of Indian-tanned moosehide for the foot part, and hair-sealskin for the tops. Moccasins should be made of native smoke-tanned moose, deer, or caribou hide whenever available. Commercial types are soft-tanned cowhide or horsehide for the foot part and split leather for the top.

Moccasins or mukluks should never be worn indoors on cabin floors, because the soles become compressed, not only causing them to lose their insulating quality, but making them smooth and dangerously slippery on packed snow or ice. The trouble with commercial moccasins is that the smooth grain surface of the skin is not removed in the tanning process, and thus they become very slippery. They are not nearly as warm as Indian-tanned caribou or moosehide. Roughening the bottoms of com-

Commercial cowhide moccasin

mercial moccasins with very coarse sandpaper helps somewhat to overcome the smooth grain.

The army mukluk, sold in surplus, made with white leather for the foot part and canvas for the tops, has the same slipping problem. I cemented moosehide, flesh side down, with shoemaker's cement, to the bottoms, which overcame this problem and made this surplus item valuable footwear.

A number of economical mukluk adaptations can be made, such as moosehide or buckskin for the foot part and canvas for the tops. If desired, in order to stiffen and keep the tops up, the canvas fabric can be filled with thinned varnish or clear lacquer, even paraffin melted and dissolved in naphtha gas. Canvas uppers are then about as satisfactory as sealskin.

Due to compression underfoot, wool felt inner soles can be added for additional warmth, but these should be made from rather flexible material to avoid flatness underfoot. Such flat-

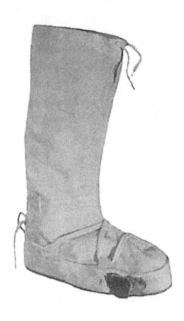

*Army mukluk with sole and loop added
for attaching snowshoe harness or hitch*

ness destroys much tactility; in short, you lose part of the foot
"feel" on ice and snow.

Socks of the common knitted variety should be of heavy-
weight wool, reaching just under the knees. Length of trip will
determine how many pairs needed, but plan on at least a pair
for each week of wear if travel is on snowshoes or on foot. At
extremely low temperatures, when you also wear a combination
of one pair of wool socks with two pairs of duffels in moccasins
or mukluks, then you should have four pairs of duffel socks
in all.

10

THE FUNCTION
OF WINTER CLOTHES

It may seem presumptuous to tell anyone *how* to wear clothes, yet winter wilderness clothing, no matter how scientifically developed, will be less functional if it is not worn according to a set of principles long established in the field.

Exploration and general wilderness travel have proved that the fewer clothes one can wear with reasonable comfort during strenuous physical activity, the better. Since it is possible to avoid the constant enemy of the winter trail—perspiration—only to a limited degree, the experienced wilderness traveler cuts back on his dress until he is apt to be more on the cool than on the warm side of comfort. Of course, it goes without saying that when stops are made on the trail, or when riding on a dog sled or motorized toboggan, one cannot don too many clothes.

In order to better understand the function of winter clothing we need to be concerned with the difference between high-

and low-density materials. For example, an inch-thick plate of steel has a high density and, therefore, is a poor insulator. But shred the steel, say into #ooo steel wool an inch thick, and you have low-density material and, therefore, a good insulator.

Laboratory testing of insulating materials can be highly important if the basic factors discovered are subsequently given exhaustive tests in the field. We know, for example, by laboratory tests, that if in low-density material we can trap air in numerous tiny voids, we have a good insulation principle. This is quite academic when we are insulating some inanimate object, such as a refrigerator.

In the insulation of clothing, however, we have a far more complex problem. Just the normal function of the skin gives off more than a pint of water a day by the drying of the skin alone, over and above perspiration. Therefore, when insulating clothing we must not wholly prevent air from circulating as we do in the insulating of a refrigerator. Air must be trapped in the tiny voids of our clothing insulation only long enough to permit this air to absorb whatever moisture it can from the body. The porousness and low density of our insulated clothing should then be such as to allow as much air as possible slowly to move out through our clothing and be replaced with drier air. The bellows action created from body activity brings about this exchange if clothing is right in principle; that is, of *porous* and *low-density* materials. Such ventilation if too rapid will chill the body; if too slow will cause serious condensation and destroy the insulating value of our clothing. (The colder the weather the drier the air, a factor working to our advantage.) In the meantime the burning of food in the body (metabolism) is producing heat to warm the replaced air. Thus, we are able to keep the air-replacement process constant.

Laboratory testing of clothing insulating materials can be deceptive. Such tests have shown that if you keep the same low density in any of the materials used for trapping dead air in numerous minute voids, not much difference exists in the insulating value of one material compared to another. This can give false encouragement to the making of winter garments with lower-grade insulating materials, to the final dismay of the user. In fact, if you try out two *new* quilted garments—one of cotton, the other of goose down—of the same thickness and density at the same temperature, humidity, and wind velocity, you will not at first see much insulating difference. The deception here lies in the fact that when the garments are first worn, the density of the quilted materials will for a short time remain the same. To determine why a garment made of quilted, Northern goose down is far superior to one of quilted cotton or other low-grade filler in the same initially created density, roll both garments tightly and store them in this manner for a while. Afterward shake both garments vigorously to fluff the filler.

What happens? The cotton filler remains compressed while the goose down readily fluffs. As you continue to wear the garments, the goose down will increase its fluff, while the cotton will compress even more, and by reason of this compression, will have less and less insulating value as the cotton increases in density with continued use. Also, as the body gives off moisture, any increased density caused by compression will reduce the chance of moist air leaving the garment, thus further reducing its insulating value. The moisture becomes a rapid conductor of heat, and the wearer feels cold.

What we need then for good insulation of the human body is low-density material that will remain so, such as goose down. But just as important, we need *thickness* that by its natural fluff quality will remain thick.

For comfort under the same low-temperature conditions, you could, roughly speaking, use insulation four inches thick while sitting on a motorized toboggan, one-half-inch thick when running behind a dog team. The more active you are the greater the metabolism and the less insulation you require.

We cannot, of course, prescribe the wearing of a particular garment thickness for a certain degree of temperature. The reason is that the chill factor affecting body comfort may vary with the same temperature. The chill factor is based on degree of temperature, wind velocity, and humidity. And along with these we need to consider three other factors: the quality of blood circulation in the wearer, his metabolism, and the degree of physical activity he is expending. Because of these variables we are compelled to depend largely on the feel of the individual traveler as to how much clothing to wear; on his good judgment to shed garments before he experiences perspiration problems; and, of course, to don them again before he feels too cold.

Short pants need simple fastening devices for quick donning and removal. A pair of generous tapes to tie or a Velcro lap is best for holding them up. After donning them, the parka is also slipped on and the *assumption sash* (any tie cord, thong, or band) is tied around the waist to keep cold air from coming up underneath the parka shirt. (Some parkas have an adjustable draw-cord built into the garment.) Assumption sashes are often made highly decorative, lending a colorful note of contrast to trail dress.

Even in extremely cold weather, perspiration can accumulate. It develops in the form of rime between garments and greatly reduces their insulating value. The imperative need for drying garments and sleeping bag in camp at every opportunity cannot be overemphasized.

In early arctic exploration, most expeditions were planned for light travel by including only enough liquid fuel for cooking. With limited fuel, no drying of garments and sleeping gear was possible. As time went on, both clothes and sleeping gear became filled with accumulated rime. Members of certain expeditions, weary with fatigue and lack of sleep from cold sleeping bags, suffered a general functional depression, and froze to death in their sleeping bags. Later in exploration procedure, stations were established along the route in order that fuel could be freighted in relays by dog team to the advance party. While this plan was much costlier, requiring more men and equipment, it was a great turning point in exploration history. When members could sleep comfortably in daily-dried, warm sleeping bags, and also travel in dry clothes, exploration began to show a higher degree of success and had remarkably few fatalities. In recent years, of course, mechanical equipment has again altered exploration methods, but where there is also physical activity—and there still is despite the mechanical means—the same general principles of drying bedding and clothing apply.

Definite provision should, therefore, be made for drying sleeping gear and clothes on a ridge line in the upper inside of the tent when travel is beyond the tree line on the Barrens or sea ice. If one has a notion of freeze-drying clothes in the open air as our grandmothers did, remember that it takes about five days to dry a handkerchief at 40 below zero. In forest travel, even though the equipment on hand consists of tent and stove, it should be borne in mind that a large, open, auxiliary fire can be maintained for drying out. Underwear may be laundered on the winter forest trail and dried before the large open fire, but not readily dried in a tent, except with an extended layover. Generally one has to be content with keeping garments dry of perspiration when limited to drying them in a tent.

When retiring for the night, always crawl into a dry sleeping bag with thoroughly dry underwear and socks on. This is accomplished by donning the suit of underwear and socks worn the day before, even though unlaundered but dried. (Pajamas are excess and should not be carried.) The following night one dons the unlaundered suit of underwear worn the day before, etc. If this seems nonhygenic, bear in mind that in the clean cold and snow of the winter wilderness, you do not have the hygenic problem experienced in conventional indoor life. Moreover, you don't have to be concerned with a prissy standard of fastidiousness on the winter trail. When you do reach a Hudson's Bay Post, a cabin shelter, or a forest area of ample fuel where a large open fire can be built, it is important to do a laundry, not so much for the luxury of cleanliness but to rid underwear of the accumulated perspiration salt increment that in varying amounts robs clothing of its original, maximum warmth and softness. Salt also tends to draw moisture to itself.

Eskimos in earlier years, and some now, use fur next to the skin. Such garments have a double fur facing so that upon the accumulation of perspiration the inner fur facing is turned outward. The perspiration freezes into rime and is then beaten off or allowed to rub and dry off. By repeating this process at daily intervals, the perspiration problem is rather uniquely controlled. In both white and Eskimo camps, lice in fur clothing can become a problem. It was readily solved by the Eskimo who left his clothing out of doors for a while in extremely low temperatures. The lice froze hard and were easily shaken out of the garments. In summer he lays lice-infested garments on an anthill. The ants soon have all the lice.

Eskimos generally sleep in the nude—an accomplishment I have not succeeded in imitating with complete comfort. No doubt it has advantages, but when getting in and out of bed, and especially if one must get up at night, the protection of clothes is essential.

Whenever *underwear* is mentioned herein, it has specific reference to those garments worn *next* to the skin which take up the immediate perspiration. When *undergarments* are mentioned, reference is confined to those garments worn over the underwear and under the parka—in short, the in-between garments.

Outer garments, such as parka and short pants, that are alternately removed and donned along the trail are tucked securely, never carelessly, under the pack ropes on a dog sled or motorized toboggan trailer. If travel is afoot with a pack, top

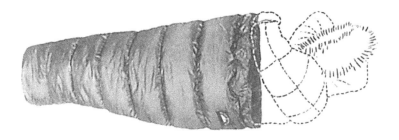

Ultra-light sleeping equipment using down half-bag and parka

garments are carried strapped outside of the pack to be readily available when needed, because stops and rests are frequent. Where travel is by saddle horse and packhorse train, there is generally little need to remove the parka and short pants at all. In the saddle, the short pants are worn under the chaps. Parkas for use in a saddle should either be shorter than ordinary or should have a drawstring on the lower edge of the skirt for blousing and tying around the waist.

If we practice the same fortitude in removing garments on the winter trail that some of us practice in the cold morning shower in the city, perspiration problems are much reduced. The procedure used is to leave camp clad in full dress, short pants, parka, and assumption sash, unless the initial body-warming activity around camp does not warrant it. Once on the trail, begin by removing the assumption sash at the first sign of generating the least physical warmth; then, loosen the parka at the neck and throw back the hood, under which will be a ski or stocking cap. Finally, before full comfort is felt, remove the short pants and parka entirely. The thin, high-count-material anorak or windbreaker with a hood and fur ruff, described in the previous chapter, is then slipped on over the undergarments—temperatures and wind, of course, determining and regulating all of these various adjustments to fit the existing conditions and the individual's cold resistance. The point is to avoid perspiration without ever becoming *too* cold.

Mountain climber's "bootee" for night wear

In mountain climbing and other winter travel afoot, every conceivable effort should be made to reduce weight. Here the parka and short pants are put into service as a part of the sleeping equipment, using what is called a half-bag, elephant boot, elephant sock, etc. This is generally a down bag that reaches just above the waistline. The short down parka used for day travel, fully as thick as the half-bag, is then put into use to supply the upper part of the sleeping combination. This short down parka and half-bag complement is available commercially for this purpose. Quilted down so-called bootees replace the footwear worn during the day, and add to foot warmth at night. Various duffel or felted Finn socks, previously mentioned, can also be used for this purpose. Since no vision, obviously, is required at night, the parka hood is drawn well down around the face, allowing just enough of an opening for a breathing space; the half-bag is closed around the waist with a drawstring; mittens are slipped on, and one is prepared for the night. If desired, arms can be withdrawn from the sleeves and kept inside the parka; it adds somewhat to body warmth.

Winter tragedies caused by improper equipment have not been few. It might be of some value here to suggest what *not* to wear. When I mentioned to a winter trail companion that four-buckle overshoes should be worn over duffel socks for all but the lower temperatures, he suggested that felt overshoes had been worn over soled felt shoes or work shoes for many decades. But the felt-shoe-overshoe combination so increases the size and weight of the overshoe as to make it a clumsy, serious handicap, wearying over the miles of trail. It is understandable how exhaustion can overcome anyone using this equipment long before the day is half over. The combination of overshoe and felt shoe generally belonged to the farmer or heavy-equipment operator who sat for hours on a wagon seat or tractor. Here the combination is wholly satisfactory. It has no place in breaking a winter trail where nimble footing is needed. The gigantic-sized, soled, white felt "bunny boots" sold in army surplus are in this same clumsy category. A soldier on guard duty or on roads in combat service does very well with them, and they are ideal for ice fishermen who are inactive; but over twenty miles of wilderness trail, the result is discouraging. By wearing lightweight, four-buckle overshoes directly over duffel socks, you can gain minimum size and weight in footwear, comparable to mukluks or moccasins, giving a high degree of mobility.

Fashionably cut garments made principally for resort skiing should never be used on the long wilderness trail. They do not possess the attributes required for winter camp activity and travel. A woman, especially, is prone to the use of ski clothes and other fancy dress for winter trail activity. As we might say, she may gain a romantic point with John Doe, but she is sure to lose out with Jack Frost.

In fact, all of the trussing and girdling devices, along with the cosmetics, that women wear should be left at home, or stored at the embarkation point until the conventional deception game starts again back at the road- or railhead. These contraptions not only restrict body movement, they are circulation killers, and cut down on the insulation efficiency of properly applied winter garments. Cosmetics increase the possibility of facial frostbite, while hand lotions tend to reduce hand warmth.

What should a woman wear on the winter wilderness trail? She will not go far wrong, I have concluded, if she will adopt in principle a man's clothes. Her trousers can be custom-made on the free cut of a man's but with the opening at the sides. And if she insists on zippers, she should add buttons or Velcro in the event of zipper failure. The greatest common mistake women make in selecting a man's style of trail clothes for themselves is that they insist on getting these clothes in a size small enough to emphasize their body contours. If, temporarily, they will forego glamour, they will have no special problem on the trail.

Many firms have recently been engaged in the development of improved winter clothes, among them the Research and Development Command of the Military Services. Unless one has experienced the light, free, highly technical winter trail garments of recent development, one can't conceive of the advantages gained. It is now possible to purchase stock items that are very satisfactory, although these items are not commonly sold in retail clothing stores. Much of the trade is on a maker-to-consumer basis. This gives direct, personal contact of user with maker, and allows for some remodeling of stock garments as well as the custom-making of others to fit the personal needs of those experienced in wilderness travel. Where commercial firms do not custom-make garments, consideration should be given to the remodeling of such garments by local alteration and tailor shops.

The winter clothing and sleeping gear that I used nearly a half century ago was purchased in part from natives in the Northern forests and arctic regions. Mittens, mukluks, and duffel socks I usually made myself. The caribou parka was a frequent purchase since it tended to shed badly, and therefore was rather short-lived. Also, due to only a partial tanning process by the natives, the parkas had the unpleasant odor of carrion in any but low temperatures. Usually, these half-tanned parkas had to be hung outside the tent in a high place away from the appetite of sled dogs. Eventually, I tried August-killed caribou skins commercially tanned and then returned them to the natives to be made into parkas. It helped some but still they were not wholly satisfactory due to continued shedding of hair.

Hair-sealskin mukluks with square flipper sealskin for soles have been available from the Hudson's Bay Company outpost stores, and in some regions at the time of this writing, still are. The Indian-tanned, soft, porous "buckskin" shirt usually was a valuable addition to any outfit if the shirt was of simple pattern, comfortably large, and the "gingerbread" fringes were left off. One of the shirt's greatest virtues lay in the fact that it never seemed to wear out, for many of us a real economy. Unlike commercial-leather jackets, the buckskin shirt, being porous and soft, like cloth, allows the body to breathe, and therefore is warm and relatively free from condensation difficulty. Common leather jackets are unsatisfactory cold-weather garments, because they rapidly conduct heat from the body and increase condensation. Also, buckskin jackets from commercially tanned hides are unsatisfactory unless the surface grain can be removed in the manner of native-tanned hides.

While these early clothing items supplied by natives left something to be desired, they were far superior to the items then available on the commercial market. The sheepskin coats and mackinaws, lumberjack rubber-bottom, leather-top footwear, chopper mitts with knit liners, and cap with fur earlaps of that period, while barely passable in the logging camps, proved to be items of despair on the winter exploration trail. It was clumsy, restricting clothing that many used on ventures such as gold rushes and other expeditions that contributed to much discomfort and caused so many casualties. A number of these items are still "standard" for the cold regions—equipment that should discourage the most zealous outdoor winter enthusiast.

Was it any wonder that earlier, competent leaders of expeditions resorted almost solely to the use of Eskimo and Indian dress to accomplish anything worthwhile in exploration?

While commercial items are now available in excellent materials and design, men of long training in the field are inclined to have their items altered somewhat. Quilted down undergarments are very satisfactory. These can be had from stock and should not be selected in too skimpy a size. Bind or restriction must be carefully watched, to get a size that will allow full freedom of body movement. There is less danger of error in the selection of too large than too small a size. What may seem to be a proper size when first tried on, becomes too small when the garment adjusts to the wearer after what might be described more as retraction than shrinkage once the garment has been given rough use on the trail. The "preshrunk" label on a garment should not always be taken too literally.

Mittens, as described in Chapter 9, need to be large enough for free action of the hands. As I have pointed out earlier, if there is any bind at all at the back of the hand when the fist is clenched, the mittens are too small. Any mitten bind also reduces the insulating value.

If the reader will write to me in care of the publisher, I will give an available source for special items at the time of the reader's communication to me. Ski and mountain climbing footwear should be selected from firms specializing in this equipment.

11

WINTER WILDERNESS
TRAVEL METHODS

PART 1 / Dog Sled and Hand-Drawn Units

IN the early part of the century, before the advent of airplanes, motorized toboggans, and snowmobiles, every enterprising winter wilderness traveler was the proud owner of a dog team. A well-bred, properly trained sled dog could on occasion bring as much on the wilderness market as an average saddle horse in cattle country.

Those whose budget would not allow the price of a dog team, or who found it difficult to maintain a team throughout the year, made out quite well by stopping over at such gateway-to-the-wilderness cities as Winnipeg, Quebec, and Seattle, where it was possible with a few days' scrounging around to pick from the streets a strange assortment of canines, owned or ownerless, for a team. Dog snatching from the streets was not at that time—at least by the snatchers—regarded as a crime, but rather as a necessity and convenience. Later, the dogs were often set free again in their original locale, not particularly through a guilty conscience or compassion for the dogs and their owners, we may be sure, but because there was not a convenient and economical way of keeping the dogs through the summer, unless they could be turned loose on some fairly large island far from shore to forage for themselves. Dogs so treated grew thin and gaunt but were systematically fed and made ready for harness as winter again approached.

Dogs snatched from city streets apparently liked the adventure that went with wilderness travel, though some with poor hair and feet fared badly. Later, when such dogs were released in their original city neighborhoods after having spent a winter on the trail, they would affectionately follow their unrequiting winter master to the rail station and chase the accelerating train until utter exhaustion left them sprawling behind in despair. During the Klondike gold rush, no dog owner in a Pacific port city could expect his pet "pooch," if he looked at all serviceable, to live out a metropolitan life of ease. A dog's chance of winding up on the shores of Lake LaBarge or in a Klondike gold wash was almost a foregone conclusion. Some even wound up as food, when mere survival became the overriding consideration.

Despite the advent of mechanization, dog teams are still widely used in the North, both in the forest and on the Barrens. A few years ago, on arriving after dark at Moose Factory on the shore of James Bay, I found an outdoor hockey game in progress between members of the Hudson's Bay Company and the Indian Hospital staff. Whenever an outstanding play had aroused the spectators to shouts of applause, every dog in the Indian village gave forth with a concerted, complementary howl. The ensuing chorus from hundreds of these sled dogs was a magnificent, wolfish, primitive, booming crescendo of sound.

The term "thoroughbred" as applied to dogs is bandied

The traditional sled dog of the North

about with a recklessness that needs some down-to-earth analysis. The ancestry of the dog is still pretty much in dispute, but we find the broadest information indicating that the prime origin was in the wolf, the fox, the hyena, and other creatures capable of entering the breed. "Dog" is a man-controlled breeding concept. Actually, there is no such thing as a true, natural dog—a matter which many will consider as a juggling of semantics. Most sled dogs used in the North are in part related to the wolf, and like the wolf, in many instances, howl rather than bark. Some believe that this common trait of howl-ing rather than barking is the only similarity and that the wolf blood is quite absent, but this is perhaps a form of wishful thinking which has little basis in fact. That the traditional sled dog of the North, the husky, has a tail that turns over his back while the wolf's arcs low has been used to discredit wolf ancestry in these animals. In any event, no matter what senti-ment exists for the purebred notion, a vast number of sled dogs have been and are successfully bred with wolves.

Sled dogs are thus essentially breed mixtures. Despite the avid arguments on the part of many to give thoroughbred identification to their own splendid dogs, we may assume that by a process of breeding in which various dogs of individual qualities are combined with the wolf and other creatures, a sort of breed has resulted needing no defense against the charge of mongrelism. He is in a category isolated enough to give generic sense to the terms "husky," "Samoyed," "mala-mute," and some other basic names less in the public mind. It seems to me of little consequence what the origin or ancestry is, so long as a good end product results, and there *are* some extraordinarily fine specimens throughout the world. The term "mongrel" has thus become needlessly disparaging. The more logical and praiseworthy reference should be hybridism, a pro-cess in both plant and animal crossing that has brought results superior to "thoroughbred."

Harness-dog breeders must, of course, take into considera-tion the environmental and circumstantial need. To combine strength, speed, proper hair covering, size, good feet, stamina, and such qualities as will permit the animals to survive the rigors of a particular climate and rugged terrain, breeding must go on with infinite patience. One litter I tried came through as excellent sled dogs, except that so little hair was on their ears that they froze in cold weather, and the breeding process in this case had to be continued until proper hair cov-ering, along with other qualities, was developed.

The fact that sled dogs are bred with wolves does not de-preciate the value of sled dogs as congenial animals. Dogs with 50 per cent wolf blood have performed in harness and made the domestic adjustment of dogs with little or no recent wolf breeding.

The handling of dog behavior is the basis for as much argument through the long Northern night as breeding and harnessing methods. A rough division might be made between those drivers who practice tolerance and love for their dogs and those who think they must assert their virility by beating dogs into submission. The fallacy of spare the whip and spoil the child corresponds to the adage of spare the whip and spoil the dog. The matter of categorical division in either instance should not be difficult. Where there is a shortage of intelligent direction, there must, I suggest, be a compensating extension of the whip method to bridge this tragic gap. It seems to apply as well to horses and dogs as to children. Both the whip method and the intelligent influence method work their own particular ends, but the results differ widely. Kindly handled dogs, for example, have been appraised at a market value considerably higher in price than whip-handled dogs. This should supply an answer for those who think beating in any sense is essential to training.

The pseudo-romance of wilderness fiction has built up a false notion of savagery among huskies and other types of dogs. Sled dogs, I have found, reflect pretty much the character of owner and driver. Many sled dogs are abused—often deposited, as I have already mentioned, on some island in summer to starve or to forage for themselves. Some, though systematically fed, are still constantly abused. Thus, they sometimes develop what might seem to be a savage nature. When sled dogs are well fed, kindly treated, and otherwise properly cared for, they are friendly to man, even though they lustily battle among themselves. Not often do they bite man. It can happen when they are excited while fighting, and instinctively if their food is interfered with. In some extremely rare cases, children have been mauled by sled dogs where the children have stumbled or been thrown to the ground in rough play. There seems to be a natural and uninhibited tendency in dogs of certain breed to rush upon a creature falling to the earth, based apparently on the inherent, wild-hunt instinct.

Sled dogs can become pets just as do other dogs. However, for practical reasons, it has not been considered wise to display affection for dogs while they are in harness. Affection should be shown before or afterward. The best-disciplined dogs, I have found, are those where a kindly and not an overaffectionate relationship exists between dogs and driver while on the trail. This is not easy, of course, in general practice. These animals have a way of capturing your affection, and to refrain from an occasional caress is difficult. A soft-spoken, kindly remark after a heavy haul, or where the dogs have done something that prompts a rewarding caress, is good practice. It alleviates the pressure put on the dogs during the drive, and recaptures their confidence in the driver.

My first experience in the use of a whip was the last. I was crossing a wilderness lake when a fresh track in the snow and a shadowy figure in the distance revealed a timber wolf just about to enter some shore cover. And at that precise moment, not being held by the sled brake, the team was off like a flash. As an old saying goes, if lightning were possible in this subzero weather, it would have had to "strike twice" to hit that streaking team.

I found the dogs a short time later. The Peterborough toboggan was wedged in between two trees, and the dogs were clawing the snow and chewing their harness to be free for the chase. One at a time, I took a whip to the dogs.

The dogs' expression of despair and their reaction to this whipping was more than I expected. When they reached the lake, they went on what might best be called a "slowdown" strike. They hung their heads. I had never whipped them before. In fact, the idea of whipping dogs was so repulsive to me, as I had so often seen it administered, that I made up my mind that it would never again happen in my practice. I was, no doubt, a bit weary from long trail travel, and while in low temper was provoked into the whipping—the way whippings anywhere are usually provoked—calculated corporal discipline without anger being pretty much a face-saving, pretentious fallacy.

I felt worse when a couple of the dogs dodged repeatedly as I went to make up for my bad conduct with kindly caresses. They seemed to expect a second flogging. It was plain to see that they, as well as I, were thoroughly unhappy over the whole affair.

Instead of attempting to drive the dogs from their slowdown strike, I started off down the lake, giving one short, subdued call. Slowly but reluctantly, they rose and followed. Perhaps I imagined much of it, but it seemed the dogs were never again as free with me, or as high-spirited.

Dog whips are becoming less popular, due, no doubt, to the influence of better drivers who have shown that whips are unwarranted and that superior harness dogs are developed by kindly and considerate treatment. Among the whip-hand drivers it was popular to be able to wield a long blacksnake whip in such fashion as to nip a straggler. The practice looked romantic in the movies. But blacksnake whips had two results, creating bad-tempered animals and more frequent dogfights. Often a straggler when he felt the sting of a whip would apparently assume that he was being nipped by the teeth of another dog. A fight would ensue, most often involving the whole team in a bloody melee, and sometimes the loss or temporary crippling of a dog or two.

Since dogfights are much like the traditional Donnybrook Fairs practiced by people heavy on muscle and light on gray matter, dogs will take part in any nearby fight. There is a grave danger that several dogs will pick on one and kill it before the fight can be stopped.

I have seen many methods of stopping dogfights—none very effective. The whip is not an effective treatment. A club administered to fighting dogs is liable to injure them seriously. A man trying to stop a fight is apt to be taken for a participant and can become injured, although one usually has to take this risk.

Snowshoes rammed down between fighting dogs has some effect in cramping their belligerent style.

Where dogs are staked out and have a tendency to fight, I place contesting dogs close to each other on long, individual leashes attached to their collars, looping the other end of the long leash through a small sail pulley hung on the limb of a tree. At the first sign of a fight, I take hold of the remote end of the leash and hoist their front quarters off the ground where they can carry on only "oral combat" until they develop an indissoluble association between fighting and taking an upward cooling-off swing. It is in no way physically impairing and has a beneficial effect in reducing their belligerency. A strange dog added to a team generally poses a problem, and he must be protected from the other dogs for a while until he finds himself accepted.

Many trappers in the North often employ only two rather large dogs to haul their loads over the trap line. It isn't impractical or undignified for a man to lend a hand in general hauling or to boost a sled or toboggan over bad places. On lakes, rivers, and other level areas where the going is easy, the size of the load hauled by a few harness dogs is often amazing to the person who first sees them in action.

One night I reached a lake region from the railroad with a single Mackenzie River malamute, a Peterborough toboggan, and a load of supplies weighing slightly under 250 pounds. Two additional dogs that had been left with a trapper friend were to be picked up the following day. However, it was late, and anxious to reach my cabin, I decided to give the new malamute, "Chinook," an assist by helping him pull the sled and thus get the load to the cabin without the immediate aid of the other dogs. A long trace was attached to the sled for me, while Chinook was put into regular harness on a second, shorter trace.

I had personally trained Chinook—brought down as a pup from the North—but had never put him to a grueling test of pulling. The going, however, was very good on the lake, due to an overflow having frozen and formed a hard sledding surface.

"Whoit!" I called to him, and we were off.

Chinook, rising on his hind legs, made a lunge forward. Finally, my only task became one of trying to keep up with him. My trace fell loosely behind and was soon coiled and laid on the load. The crunch of Chinook's feet on the snow as he pulled was marvelous to hear. Although I would not, of course, have maintained so heavy a schedule for him had I been in immediate possession of the other dogs, I did learn from his solo pull what a strong and magnificent creature he was. Later, as I collected the team, he proved to be a fine lead dog.

Two good sled dogs, or even one, can thus become a valuable asset to the wilderness dweller who needs to transport toboggan or sled loads of equipment and supplies to cabins from a landing, or for travel into the interior. A camping outfit that is light in weight but rugged and practical, plus the required amount of carefully selected provisions for both campers and dogs, is well handled by three fairly large dogs for a trip of several weeks. This will not apply to much of the rough, heavy equipment used currently, such as thick canvas tents. But by placing improvised upstands or handlebars on toboggans, dogs can be helped over difficult places. Komatiks, heavy sledges pulled by many dogs, harnessed fan-wise, used along the arctic coast, usually have upstands built in. Where toboggans are required in deep, soft snow over forest trails, one person with snowshoes needs to go ahead to break trail for the dogs.

Man will never cease to wonder at the devotion of dogs pulling loads long distances—the only reward a single meal each day often placed on the cold surface of the snow. To see tired dogs mushing along over some frozen lake expanse on a cold, crisp, starlit night, even after all-day travel, is to get one wondering with profound sympathy about these creatures who have meant so much down through the ages in the quest for exploration and adventure.

Why do they pull? How easy it would be to slack off and do only a small part of the job, or entirely refuse to pull. Yet, you see the traces usually stretched tight as these animals dutifully continue to lean into the harness long after a reasonable day's work should have ended. Is it reflex inherited from centuries of evolution in the harness? No answer will do.

When the sled has come to rest, it sometimes takes great effort to get it moving again from its inertial position, or because of runner-pressure-freeze to the ice or snow. (To avoid this freeze, the sled should be tipped on its side whenever there will be lengthy pauses and the type of load will permit.) But how understandingly the dogs solve this freeze or inertial problem. You will see them rise on their hind legs and give a lunge, with an almost uncanny knowledge it will take more than just steady pulling to get the sled in motion. And they do this before they have had any special or prolonged training. The concept of dogs overcoming inertia always amazes me, as does much of their magnificent conduct and devotion.

Although brought from the Yukon, several dogs of a team I had acquired spent their puppyhood near Minneapolis, Minnesota. Initiating them into the wilderness gave me as much pleasure as those opportunities I have had of initiating people into the wilds. The dogs could not quite make out what the thunderous rumble was on a wilderness lake when on a very cold night freezing pressure ripped the ice for miles. They would stop, prick up their ears, finally decide that nothing apparently was wrong, and then mush on. As the sound boomed directly beneath their feet, their ears would be cocked at a most amusing and inquisitive angle—somewhat like robins feeding on a lawn. An owl calling from the shore would have their casual attention; but a wolf howling—as they do more frequently in February—would send them into a frenzy. Up would go their heads and ears, and from their throats would emanate a well-sustained howl, sending a reverberating echo through the frosty air from forest wall to forest wall.

Sled dogs are fed once each day toward evening, at a regular time whenever possible. This leaves them well stoked with natural furnace fuel while they sleep. Morning feeding would make them sluggish on the trail. Dog food comes in wide variety, depending on supply and circumstance.

No doubt, the best and simplest method of feeding dogs is to give each animal a pound of well-balanced dog pemmican per feeding. It is made of dried meat mixed with fat, and comes in bars of 16 cubic inches, 4″ x 4″ x 1″. The convenience of packing such compact, water-free food places it high on the list. Dogs do well on it. Dog pemmican has been the stock dog food on many expeditions and is not readily available, except on special order. Indians and Eskimos have on occasion dried and prepared it for their own dogs.

Frozen fish, portions of game not used for human consumption, and some skinned-out, trap-line carcasses are commonly fed to dogs. Because of its convenience commercial dog food is used a great deal of late. Chick-starter, rolled oats, and lard, cooked together in various combinations with rough fish and meat, are used a great deal. In earlier times much dried white-fish was fed to dogs, supplied in what was called "sticks," a dozen fish strung on a stick. When the big suckerfish run is on in the spring, tons of these can easily be netted and dried to jerked-fish hardness, ground into meal, mixed with chick-feed or other staple cereal grains, cooked, shaped into bars, and dried again. Some lard should be added in the cooking. The feeding of moose, caribou, and other wild creatures to sled dogs over the years, while quite necessary in many remote regions, seriously decimated wildlife. With the advent of the motorized toboggan, which will be treated in Part 2 of this chapter, the killing of wildlife for dog food has been greatly reduced.

During World War II, as I was about to enter the Berens

River on the east shore of Lake Winnipeg for the interior by canoe, I observed a great number of Indians gathering on the dock to meet the old, wood-burning steamer, *Kenora,* arriving from Winnipeg with a cargo. The assembly was waiting for a very important shipment of lard. Lard was needed for human consumption, of course, but the imminent demand for lard at the time was primarily for the dogs, to balance the cereal ration. Fats, being used for the making of ammunition and other products, were then in short supply.

I never feed dogs without feeling sorry for them as they ravenously bolt their meal in seconds and then sniff around for a transient crumb or two that has become detached.

Nomenclature in dog driving becomes varied according to nationality and region. The old horse driving commands: "Gee" to turn right, "Haw" to turn left, "Ho" to stop, are also commonly used in some areas to drive dogs. "Mush" to go, no doubt, came from the French *"Marche,"* common in many localities. In some parts of the Far North it is "Ouk" (right), "RRA" (left), "Hah" (stop), and "Whoit" (start). Variation of these terms and others distinctly different will appear in diverse localities, the spelling being pretty much what they sound like to you. "Whoit"—to go—is often thought to be in consonant with a whip sound, thus convincing to any hesitant straggler that has tasted of the lash. However, dogs unfamiliar with the whip come to know "Whoit" innocently, and respond to it as readily.

Harnessing methods are of wide, capricious choice, and also create arguments far into the wilderness night. The method is most generally dictated by the nature of the area traveled. It is essential on the open sea ice to harness dogs in the traditional rayed-out fan style, where every dog is on his own, individual, long trace. If there is a break through the ice, a toggle near the sled provides ready release for each dog, leaving him only his harness and a trailing trace. The trailing trace sometimes allows one to "fish" a dog out of a lead in the ice. Dogs along the

Fan-wise sled dog hitching method

forested shores of James and Hudson Bays are harnessed with a modification of the fan method, so that they can not only fan out on the ice, when they reach the narrow trails of the spruce forests, but can also travel one ahead of the other on a single trace, each trace being of a length to permit this in-line spacing. In theory one wonders how the dogs can manage to avoid getting fouled up in the traces. The secret lies in the fact that because the traces are attached to the harness at the dog's back, the traces remain high while the dogs are pulling, and

Alaskan tandem sled dog hitching method

free of their legs. When the traces do become slack, it is amazing how the dogs manage to hurdle them without tripping or altering their pace.

In the Alaska forest and mountains, the harnessing method is quite different, the common use of collars with tandem hitching being most popular.

The dog harness pattern shown in the accompanying illustration was improved by the author so that it can be adjusted to fit any size dog without stitching alteration. The straps are preferably made of folded canvas rather than webbing. These canvas folds when rounded with inserted cotton upholstery cable cord give soft, more comfortable edges to the straps. The harness is made with two straps running along the dog's back, joined together with a crosspiece at the back of the neck—the two back straps—continuing down on either side of the neck at the shoulders, crossing between the front legs, passing under the body and up the sides, joining the back straps about two thirds of the way back to a "D" ring. A snap swivel tied on one

A common dog harness improved with adjustable features by the author

end of the trace is hooked into the "D" ring, and thus quickly attaches the harnessed dog to the sled. The harness in this manner can be left on the dog. Dogs seem comfortable and work well in this harness.

When a dog's feet break through crusty snow, they are certain to become sore. Moccasins must be provided. The difficulty with moccasins made from hides is that dogs will chew them. They should, therefore, be made from canvas. While these moccasins do not wear long, they are easily made—a small bag with a drawstring at the top is all one needs. A full supply even for a long journey is light and compact to carry. They should be of light enough material and of such fit as to allow free play of the dog's feet.

Dog sleds and toboggans are also subjects of current wilderness controversy—although not to the degree of other dog driving subjects—because a choice of sled type is generally dictated by the nature of the terrain to be traveled.

On the arctic coast, Hudson Bay, James Bay, and other big-water and tundra areas, the rugged sledge (komatik), consisting of two heavy, well-turned-up plank runners held apart by spaced crosspieces bonded with rawhide, is the basic sled unit. The runners are generally iced, by first applying a humus-type mud from a bog to give bond for the icing. The mud is formed on the runners, tirelike, smoothed with a carpenter's plane, then iced by applying warm water with a woolen cloth, or, better, a piece of polar bear fur.

A brake on a sled consists of a spring pedal with teeth, driven into the ice and snow when stepped on, used mostly downhill to keep the sled from coasting over the dogs. Brakes

Wilderness toboggan showing high turn-up for mounting drifts and soft snow. (Note lashing the toboggan load.)

can be used to great advantage when dogs take a notion to be off on a wild tangent of their own.

A sled much used over the continent is the basket type. This is made in varying degrees of lightness and ruggedness—from the featherweight racing sled to heavier freighting and carriole types. It is equipped with upstands or handlebars for guiding over rough places. Often this type is equipped with steel runners, not usually iced. The runners extend out behind, where on easy going the driver can stand, hitching an occasional ride for relief. Bakelite has been found to be valuable, low-friction runner material. Fiberglas and wood impregnated with plastic

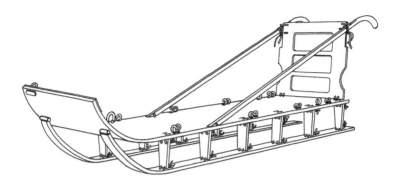

The Army convertible combination toboggan and sled unit

resins have now come into their own as runner bottoms and skis of late development.

In forest travel where there is deep snow the toboggan is the logical unit because it rides high on the snow with its large surface-bearing support area. Upstands (handlebars) are used with it, but generally these are applied by bending a green sapling or a strip of steamed, sawed lumber around the lashed load. The sapling or strip to be so bent should be covered with rags or dry moss and soaked for an hour or more with a solution of sal soda and boiling hot water until limber enough for bending. The toboggan used in forest travel is not the conventional hill-sliding type. Wilderness toboggans have a higher turn-up for mounting deep snow and drifts, as will be seen in the illustration. The turn-up is held in its arced position by two spanned rawhide thongs fastened to the first crosspiece. Here, also, the pulling traces are tied to a pivot ring, which in turn has been fastened with rawhide to the front crosspiece.

A sled popular with the Army for years can be described as a combination sled and toboggan. I purchased one of these from army surplus and found it valuable for various kinds of terrain and multiple uses. The two runners are a little wider than ski width and are mounted seven inches below a tobogganlike floor. The theory is that if the ski runners sink too deeply in the snow, the toboggan bottom with its broad bearing surface will take over and ride the snow crest. Over packed or shallow snow the runners alone, of course, will be riding the snow surface or the ice. The sled is so constructed that the runners can readily be collapsed against the toboggan bottom to give the entire unit a semblance of only a toboggan. The reason for this variable is that with runners collapsed, the toboggan adaptation will permit a much heavier load. The sled is equipped with demountable upstands (handlebars) for guiding it over rough or precarious places. Also, it has a gee pole—a pole attached to the forepart of the sled for additional control over a rough trail. This toboggan-sled, as we might call it, is primarily recommended for forest travel, although for moderate loads it can be adapted to rough sea ice travel. The outstanding feature is its versatility.

An interesting aspect of the toboggan-sled, even though commercially made for the Army, is that the parts are held together with leather thongs or rawhide in the manner of earliest construction used by Indians and Eskimos. Rawhide is not only a tough bonding material, it also provides a necessary flexibility for the integral parts of the sled. If the sled was rigidly assembled by screws and bolts without rawhide bonding flexibility, it would soon be broken up by the twisting and prying of rough trails.

One of the most interesting of all sled or toboggan units, I think, is the Indian's trapping toboggan—a very long, narrow unit, usually only about ten inches wide, and varying in length from about eight to twenty feet. The front is liberally turned up. The utility of its design is rather obvious. Since the width is extremely narrow, little snow is displaced at the front to cause resistance. It slides through narrow places in the underbrush and forest where the standard toboggan would be more apt to get hung up. Being very supple, it reminds one of a snake, undulating and conforming to every drift and ground contour.

Lone Indian trapping toboggan

It is generally drawn by one person. Every item of the load must, of course, be reduced to the narrow ten-inch width, but this is no problem with such common trapping gear as tent, sleeping bag, cooking utensils, animal skins, traps, and incidentals, all of which are individually adaptable to slim, narrow packing. (See illustration.) While essentially a trapper's innovation, it is a unit that lone winter travelers might seriously consider for pleasure or utility.

Motorized toboggan and trailer loaded with camp equipment

PART 2 / Mechanized Units

MECHANIZATION has rapidly been invading the wilderness. The motorized toboggan, autoboggan, snowmobile, whatever we choose to name it, is replacing the dog team. This may to many of us be a regrettable transition, an adjustment difficult to make. But the motorized toboggan's inevitability as a wilderness transportation vehicle stands out in stark reality over the entire world. Winston Churchill had many sympathizers for his view that the invention of the internal-combustion engine was a tragedy, as did Charles A. Lindbergh when he suggested that the plane is destroying man's most priceless possession—the wilderness itself.

Much of this may be only the nostalgia we cherish for the past. I was certain the outboard motor would impair the romance of wilderness waterways, yet, by now, most of us have readily accepted it. Like an oyster that coats an irritating grain of sand caught in its vitals, eventually to make of it a pearl, perhaps wilderness "pearls" will be made of motorized toboggans and other seeming obtrusions upon the quiet places. The first steamboat that came up the Mississippi had the people in panic that the wilderness was gone. And so it goes.

I have watched with great interest the sudden influx of many people into the winter wilderness, solely through the inception of the motorized toboggan—those who would otherwise not have stirred out of doors for winter recreation without it. Whatever instrumentation can break the barrier between indoor enervation and outdoor invigoration can be considered valuable despite the incidental lost values. The important thing to consider is that some areas should be left inviolate where mechanization is concerned, so that "silent places" for those who want serenity can continue to exist.

By virtue of the motorized toboggan a great number of people are planning winter wilderness trips. A virtual pilgrimage of young enthusiasts has beaten a path to my door for information on winter camping. This book had its nucleus before the advent of the motorized toboggan, but I am now considering that the effort expended in writing it is very timely. What apparently was needed by potential winter campers was a qualifying vehicle such as the motorized toboggan to take them out of doors.

The motorized toboggan has made changes in the lives of various peoples—urban, suburban, and wilderness citizens. Trappers who brought in their winter supplies at great cost by plane or early canoe travel are now utilizing the motorized toboggan for periodical trips to commercial centers throughout the winter for sale of fur when prices are high, for hauling supplies, and for needed social contact. Eskimos and Indians manage now to visit back and forth with friends at considerable distances. One wonders how the motorized toboggan will affect commercial plane wilderness transportation. The cost of a long wilderness trip or two by plane will just about pay for a motorized toboggan.

The basic principle in the variety of these motorized toboggans is a light rubber, or a rubber and steel caterpillar half-track, set into the floor of the unit. Motorized toboggans are ridden and controlled much in the manner of a motorcycle. They will tow a trailer toboggan or sled for hauling wilderness camping equipment and provisions. Besides the short or long wilderness trek, the motorized toboggans are used a great deal in the wilderness for various other purposes, such as the moving of fish from commercial net fishing areas to shore icing points and outbound transportation stations, the moving of items around Hudson's Bay Post from ice-based planes to warehouses, etc. On hard packed snow some travel as fast as sixty miles per hour or better, and do quite well in deep snow at lesser speeds. The motorized toboggan will part brush and get through fairly dense forest areas.

In sub-zero temperatures where water pours over lake ice from the weight of the snow, or where the tide water runs over snow-covered ice, the motorized toboggan can get into its share of trouble. The half-traction system becomes fouled up from rapidly freezing water, and there is little to be done except pitch a tent over it, or build a large open fire, for a major thawing job. This same kind of wet going can foul up a dog team, too, but the reclamation job is a little simpler. Dogs will chew out the ice from their feet in a short time and be ready to travel.

On Hudson Bay, James Bay, and other tidal waters, overflow is caused by the rising and lowering of the ice with the tide. When the tide comes in, the ice raises except where it clings to the shore. This causes a break-off about a hundred feet out. Water then spills in under the snow between the break and the shore. Since the overflow in these tidal areas is in the hundred-foot strip adajacent to the shore, one can avoid the overflow by staying farther out on the sea ice in travel along the coasts. Under these circumstances, the motorized unit should be left out on the ice, drawn up on evergreen boughs when these are available in forest areas, to keep the unit from freezing fast, the camp equipment then manually carried ashore. If the temperature is low, ice will also build up on one's waterproof footwear, and the ice will have to be cracked off by beating it with a stick.

Early, heavy snow on lakes where the ice is not yet very thick can weigh down the ice until it also causes serious overflow.

Important in both dog and motorized toboggan transportation is the study of ice conditions. Various kinds of overflow can be detected and avoided wherever there are available detours. When detours are necessary, it is amazing how well the power units will move through brush and forest where no cut trails exist, thus allowing detours when none seem available.

Slush ice can at times be removed from the half-track of motorized toboggans by lifting the rear end above the snow and "gunning" the motor. If this is done frequently, some rather precarious slush problems can often be overcome at once.

Motorized toboggans used on public roads, ditch, or shoulder must legally be fully equipped as a motor vehicle in accordance with state law. This means at least two headlights, taillight, horn, bumpers, brakes, and license plates. The driver must have a driver's license. Some states will not allow motorized toboggans on public roads.

Any mechanical device is subject to occasional failure. Accompanying motorized toboggans are instruction booklets that should be carefully studied before venturing into wilderness areas. Extra spark plugs, clutch pulley belts, incidental tools, and possible replacement parts that the manufacturer suggests carrying are points of consideration. Fuel and oil should be carried in particularly tight containers. Keep these containers

The large, enclosed, heated type snowmobile

far removed on the trailer from food items. Before leaving on a wilderness trip, it is well to make local sorties with the unit purchased, trying it out under all possible winter conditions and temperatures. One then gets the feel of the machine and learns how it will behave.

The original snowmobile, a much larger vehicle than the motorized toboggan, virtually a panel truck on a light assembly of caterpillar tread and skis, has become an important commercially made passenger and freight winter travel vehicle in the North. The caterpillar tread rides like a belt over pulleys on the surfaces of the eight-automobile-tire assembly, thus forming the traction bearing. The treads are driven by gears forward of the tires, thus turning the tread instead of the wheels. Snowmobiles can be equipped as living quarters with a heating unit, bunks, table, two-way radio, etc. The snowmobile is too wide for getting over most portage trails, which greatly limits its forest wilderness practicability, confining its use largely to sea ice or other big-water areas, rivers and to the Barrens. Two of these units should travel together for mutual aid in a breakdown. A break through the ice, because of its housed-in passengers, may result in drowning. Travel with open motorized toboggans and trailers used in combination with a pitched camp, therefore, offers greater safety over questionable ice, and is more adaptable to narrow interior trails and most general travel.

Whenever motorized toboggans traverse questionable ice, a forest-cut pole should be lashed across the front, another lashed across the back, to suspend the unit in the event of a breakthrough.

Various homemade motorized sled and toboggan units appear in the North from time to time. One do-it-yourself device is the sled powered by a plane motor and wind prop. Old airplane engines generally get put into use for this purpose, although other standard car and utility motors will do for driving the prop. The commercial motorized toboggan is, however, rapidly replacing most homemade units.

When traveling over lake and river ice with a motorized toboggan hauling a trailer of any type (sled, toboggan, etc.), the trailer should be towed fifty or more feet behind the motorized unit in the event of a break through the ice. And when no trailer is towed, a long, heavily waxed line, No. 8 sash cord, fifty or more feet in length, should be trailed. In both instances the line will enable recovery of the motorized toboggan if the water is not too deep for the line. It will be obvious that two motorized toboggans traveling together offer a great advantage in a breakdown. Keep them at least a hundred feet apart.

An advantage gained with mechanized equipment is that in good going more than one trailer can be drawn with a single powered unit of sufficient size and horsepower, allowing rather substantial equipment to be hauled, such as a chain saw, oil heating unit, roomier double tent—almost anything desired for the additional comfort of a winter camp. Also, motorized units allow the members of the party to ride. Over portage trails where there may be unusually heavy going, the speed advantage of this unit permits quickly taking part of the load over the portage and returning for the balance.

Motorized toboggans are made in various sizes and horsepower by numerous firms. Ease of starting in cold weather, size needed for the particular trip, accessory conveniences, width of the unit for particular kinds of travel—these and other points should be studied before buying. The transfer of a motorized toboggan from city to wilderness is best accomplished with the tip-down trailer specially constructed as an accessory to the motorized toboggan unit purchased. A pickup type of truck, carryall, or other flatbed vehicle will also serve, but planks with iron cleats that can be hooked onto the bumper or tail-gate hinge of such vehicles should then be provided to serve as a loading ramp. Motorized toboggans can be carried in the roomy trunk compartment of a car if the trunk is left open, and even on boat racks on top of cars, but not with much satisfaction. They can, of course, be shipped by rail or truck line to the wilderness departure point. Allow plenty of time for their arrival.

The starting of any gasoline motor in cold weather can set up a problem. Those who have driven a car in latitudes of subzero temperatures are usually familiar with the various starting boosters, such as the use of ethyl ether compounds sprayed into the carburetor filters, or the removing of spark plugs and the spraying of such compounds directly into the cylinders. These same compounds can be used for the starting of motors in toboggans. Quick-starting compounds to be poured into the gas tank should also be considered. Follow closely the directions given on the containers. For the warm-up, a motorized toboggan can, of course, be brought directly into a heated tent, once the camp gear has been removed.

Gasoline shipped into the North generally comes in drums that set outdoors where often water condenses and gets into the gas. Also, scale sloughs off from inside the metal drums.

Unfiltered gas, therefore, becomes one of the greatest problems in operating motorized toboggans, and such gas should always be filtered through a filter funnel or through a discarded felt hat.

At the risk of repeating, may I give a safety summary here as a final note: A motorized toboggan with one or two people on it is a highly concentrated load. This fact should be kept in mind, since the undersurface of the ice is often eroded by the movement of the water, causing weak spots in ice that otherwise would be of ample thickness. There is little warning when a loaded motorized toboggan goes through the ice, usually no time to leap to safety. It sinks instantly. The carrying of slim poles when walking on ice and the need to lash a pole front and back on a motorized toboggan have been suggested earlier. When riding on a toboggan over ice, both of these precautions should be taken. Carry a pole across your lap at right angles to the length of the toboggan; and if the toboggan should break through, you can grab the pole to span the ice for a climb to safety. As mentioned earlier, a waxed rope at least fifty feet long should be dragging behind the toboggan, or the trailer should be towed that far behind. Where unusually deep water areas are to be traveled over, be even more generous with the length of the trailer rope.

The need for two motorized toboggans to travel well apart over ice will be obvious as a safety factor. A set of small triple pulley blocks, or a pulley type of hoist, should be carried as a part of each motorized toboggan's equipment for use as block and tackle. If a toboggan goes through the ice and you are in a forested region, use the following method for raising the sunken toboggan: Cut three poles about three inches in diameter at the butt and ten feet long. Lash these poles together at the small ends. This will provide a tripod which can be set up on the ice over the breakthrough. Where each pole touches the ice, chop a pocket in the ice for the pole to set in, to prevent its slipping. The rope you would ordinarily use for pitching your tent can be used for the block-and-tackle pulleys. Fasten one end of your block and tackle to the apex of the tripod, tie the other to the trailing rope of your sunken toboggan. Proceed to lift the toboggan. If the toboggan is in deep water you will have to loop the trailing rope over the apex of the tripod and hold it there with a hitch around one of the poles, while you release the block and tackle for another purchase on the trailing rope, since your block-and-tackle lift will be only a few feet at a time. Repeat this until the toboggan is out of the water. Where the ice is unsafe around the hole, lay a number of poles spanned across the hole to work on. These can later be inserted under the toboggan for it to rest on.

The airplane, too, has changed travel in the winter North Country immeasurably. When the ice starts to form on waters, the switchover from float pontoons to skis begins. An interval in the switchover interrupts all flying except for helicopters, until a solid freeze-up occurs for ski-landing planes on snow-covered lake ice. Some winter flying problems are encountered, such as the icing of wings, difficult starts where warm-up appliances are needed, questionable moorings, blizzards, refueling, etc., but on the whole, winter flying is now carried on pretty much routinely.

In my early winter travel, trails became rather long in reaching the remote interior areas of special interest and activity. Now, one can load a team of dogs and sled into a chartered plane, or carry a motorized toboggan on the undercarriage of a chartered plane, and make a substantial flight to the desired area where only local travel need be carried on with motorized toboggan or dog sled. The motorized toboggan can, of course, be used to reach remote areas in amply fast time.

Where heavy loads of equipment need to be moved into the wilderness, as, for example, complete building material for a cabin, trading post, Indian school, or other development, the caterpillar train is employed. This usually consists of a standard tractor, pulling a train of horse-drawn-type bobsleds, a closed-in trailer on such sled runners bringing up the rear, provided with bunks and cooking and eating facilities, along with heating equipment.

The concentrated, heavy weight of cat-train tractors has caused some serious ice breakthroughs into wilderness lakes over the years. For this reason, drivers are not legally permitted the use of protective heated cabs on these tractors. Thus, tractor driving, without comfort of the early, heated cab, becomes a cold job in the sub-zero temperatures of the Northern wilderness. The only relief held out is when the driver can periodically run to the rear cook car and "coffee-up." However, electrically heated boots and suits are now being used by some drivers, along with various other heating devices.

12

EQUIPMENT
IN GENERAL

THE particular purpose and general nature of a winter wilderness journey will, of course, determine the list of equipment. The occasional trip, for example, will not in most instances warrant the owning and feeding of a dog team. But you can, of course, own a hand-hauled toboggan or a motorized toboggan and a winter camp outfit since these will readily store. Dog teams or motorized toboggans and their drivers, serving also as guides, are usually available for hire in wilderness areas where they are employed periodically on trap lines, on mining projects, and various other enterprises.

Sleeping equipment might best be of down or fur. When exclusively of fur, it should be double-faced, so that fur is both inside and outside the bag. The Eskimo has an ingenious method of alternately turning his fur bag inside out daily, first to freeze the nightly accumulated perspiration and then to beat off the resulting rime. By this method, he always has reason-

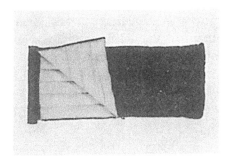

Down sleeping unit

ably dry sleeping gear. This, of course, would apply only to fur, not to down. A down bag should also be turned inside out daily, but it needs to be dried in a heated tent or outside before an open fire.

Down sleeping equipment has become the all-around choice of late, and is commercially available in a variety of styles and thicknesses. The mummy-type sleeping bag is commonly presumed to be the warmest because it has the least volume to heat up by the body. On this point, opinions differ somewhat. An objection is that its tubelike shape causes it to bridge here and there, forming cold-air pockets that must be heated by the body; whereas the rectangular-type sleeping bag or robe with its broader draping facility tends to lie down more snugly against the sleeper. Some object to the mummy type because with its cramped space it is difficult to get in and out of and does not allow the freedom of body movement enjoyed in the rectangular bag or robe. The mummy bag, of course, is much lighter in weight and takes up less room in the pack. Both types are practical, the points of difference being more or less negligible, especially since a number of modified types between the mummy and the rectangular shapes are now being made to offset some of these differences, with a compromise in features of both bags.

The question of what thickness of sleeping bag to choose

brings on a great deal of controversy and some roughly com-
puted generalizations. Various firms endeavor to give sleeping
bag thickness relative to temperature. They average out about
as follows: one inch minimum thickness at 50 degrees above
zero Fahrenheit, four inches minimum thickness at 50 degrees
below zero Fahrenheit, and intermediate thicknesses deter-
mined from this scale. These factors are based on the premise
that you are in an unheated tent and there is no perceptible
movement of air over the bag. But, since temperatures vary
from day to day, and any tenably maintained winter camp
would be provided with a heated tent, the figures become
rather ambiguous. The point to remember is that well-
recognized makers of down sleeping bags usually list them in a
wide range of thicknesses from the thinnest warm-weather
types to the thickest for extreme winter conditions. For sub-
zero camping the thickest commercial down bag should be
chosen.

Air mattresses will provide greatly increased under-body insulating value if the tubes are slit open at the valve end of the
mattress and a small quantity of goose down is inserted. Just
barely enough down should be used when fully fluffed to fill
completely the air spaces of a properly inflated air mattress.
Too much down would prevent the mattress from being easily
deflated for convenient transportation. A fairly good idea of
the amount of down required can be had by filling a fruit jar
with down, a little at a time, and shaking the jar to determine
what amount of fully-fluffed down will fill the jar. The jar can
then be laid along the tube as a rough multiple factor to determine the approximate amount of down required for the mattress. If the down contained in the one jar is carefully weighed
on a delicate apothecary scale, the amount needed for the mattress tubes can be calculated. A small, porous cloth sack tied
over the inside of the inflating valve will prevent the down
from plugging the valve opening and will allow unobstructed
movement of air in and out of the mattress. The slit openings

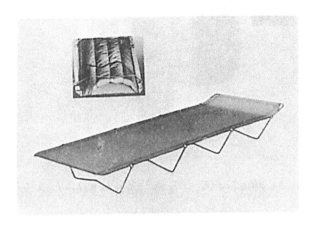

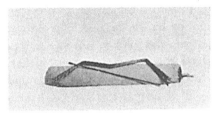

*Winter canvas camp cot. Inserts show down
underside insulation and portable feature.*

in the mattress which have been made for inserting the down
can be sealed by a strip of tire patch and cement, or simply a
piece of cotton fabric filled with rubber cement. Air mattresses
require little pressure when inflated and are, therefore, easily
mended. They should be underinflated rather than overinflated
when used, otherwise they will not allow conformity to the
body contours for fullest comfort.

A winter wilderness bed, even though inside a heated tent,
should have six inches of snow left on the ground under it, a
few inches of evergreen boughs on the snow, a waterproof
floor cloth over the boughs, a Hudson's Bay blanket or other
wool blanket over the floor cloth, a full-length air mattress over
these, and finally the sleeping bag.

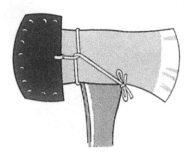

Double-bitted ax showing one blade in metal-lined sheath

A canvas cot is now being marketed that is insulated with down suspended beneath the canvas to prevent compression of the down insulation by the sleeper. The cot weighs little more than an air mattress and folds to suitable trail proportions. The difficulty involved in sleeping equipment is that body compression destroys much of the insulating value under the sleeper. Both the down-filled air mattress and the insulated cot prevent this under-body compression and may be chosen optionally with satisfaction.

The tent, previously described, is best made double; and in a size about 7' x 9' for two men, 8' x 10' for three men.

The ax needs to be double-bitted, because in extreme cold the steel may become so brittle as to break out a part of a bit. While this does not happen very often, the double-bit does raise the odds in favor of having a "spare" cutting edge. The two-and-a-half-pound blade with twenty-four-inch handle is a good trail size. The blades should be sheathed in the manner shown in the illustration. The leather pieces of the sheath are lined on the inside with thin spring brass, leather and brass all riveted together, and tied to the ax with leather thongs. Commercial all-leather sheaths are a hazard. (The butt of a single-bit ax is not required in winter because tent stakes cannot be driven.)

In forest travel, a thirty-inch, so-called Swede saw is essential. It will produce wood of proper length for the tent stove, and do it much more easily and efficiently than an ax, although an ax will also have to be carried for splitting wood, cutting tent poles, and other uses. A spare blade for the saw is important. Two types of Swedish bow saws are on the market, the best being one with a cantilever action for holding and tightening the blade without a tool. With the cantilever type, if both blades are inserted into the bow when not in use, one upside down, the blades will act as reciprocal guards during transportation. Otherwise, the sawteeth of a single blade should be protected with a folded aluminum or brass strip, tied on with a cord or thong. Collapsible saws are also available, if extreme compactness is desired. However, they do not have quite the utility and rigidity of the Swedish bow saws. The power chain saw can be a big advantage in forest travel if transportation facilities permit. The question arises whether one cares to transport the additional weight when a little muscle and a Swede bow saw will provide the necessary fuel. One is then, as Thoreau suggested, warmed twice—when cutting the wood and when burning it. However, the latest chain saws weigh only ten and a half pounds, making its choice highly attractive, especially when traveling by motorized toboggan, which also requires gas for its operation.

In describing encampments in Chapter 14, the aluminum scoop shovel is mentioned. When possible, it should be included in the equipment. Though a seemingly bulky unit, it is light, saves much labor, offers facility for a quicker-pitched, more livable camp, and more readily provides a shoveled-out camp area for freedom of movement when cutting wood, etc.

The Hudson's Bay Company sells a special ice chisel designed with a large-diameter ferrule for receiving the larger or butt end of a very long, tapering, forest-cut pole. This unit becomes valuable where, far enough north, the ice can reach a thickness of seven feet. Cutting through such ice would, of course, be done only for fishing. Melted snow can be used, or

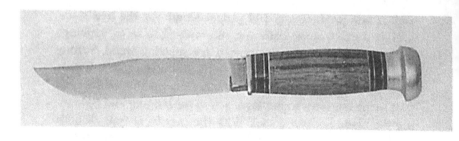

Thin blade belt knife—"Expert" pattern

ice can be cut from the surface for drinking water and cooking purposes, using a short-handled chisel, ax, or sheath knife. Melting snow for water is a much slower process than melting ice. A full pail of snow provides one tenth as much water by volume. Remember the warning about melting snow given in Chapter 2, to prevent scorching the bottom of the pail. Chain saws now have an adapter, or one can be custom-made, for boring through ice. Moderate-depth holes can also be cut with the regular chain saw itself. Because chain-sawed ice is likely to have a taint of oil or gas, such ice is generally not usable in the preparation of beverages or foodstuffs.

A belt knife properly sheathed in metal and leather as shown in the illustration is a valuable addition to the winter outfit. Avoid the thick, chisel-edged knife. The most efficient blade has a flat, continuous grind from edge to spine, the blade not too thick. The pattern shown in the illustration—a five-inch blade—is an all-around handy design. It is called "The Expert" by the maker, and fits the appellation well.

A new file will keep the saw and ax sharp and reduce labor. Canadian firms make a special ax file having alternate coarse and fine surfaces, with a convenient steel handle extension of the file blank itself. While an ordinary file is not quite the particular unit for sharpening the Swede saw, it will do for touching up, and that really is about all that is required on the trail. A round file of proper size is needed for sharpening

Belt knife sheath (brass-lined)

the chain saw. The manufacturer's pamphlet shows size and angle of file cut.

Winter camping calls for more woodcutting, of course, than mild-weather camping. Tools, therefore, need continual sharpening. The most serviceable whetstone has been somewhat alien to outdoor men—the black, gritty kind being commonly sold to them because of its low cost. Outdoorsmen who enjoy sharp, practical tools in their wilderness craft might spend a little more money to advantage by ordering a combination fine and coarse Alundum-type oilstone. This is a clean-cutting, light-brown stone made from aluminum oxide at extremely hot furnace temperatures, and is one of the hardest cutting abrasives known. It is fast cutting and does not leave the messy black residue of emery, Carborundum, and others of this black nature. With average use the stone remains flat indefinitely. A convenient and practical size is about 4" x 1½" x ¾" in a combination of coarse and fine grit, or separate grit stones can be had if desired. In addition to the Alundum stone, a small, soft Arkansas slipstone, weighing but a couple of ounces, should be added. *Soft*, as indicated here, is only a relative term, used to distinguish it from the *hard*, closer-textured, slower-cutting, fine-grained Arkansas. The soft Arkansas gives a final razor-edge touch to knife or ax. Arkansas stone is a mined, not a furnace-processed, stone. These stones, if not in local hardware store stock, can be had on special order from the manufacturer or wholesaler by any hardware or sporting goods dealer.

Stoves will be of the wood, kerosene, gasoline-primus, or propane type, depending upon the country traveled and the method of transportation. I find the airtight wood stove to be the best for forest use. Propane cannot be used below about minus 45 degrees, since it will not assume a gaseous form from

Canadian ax file

its liquefied reduction state in the tank when it is below this temperature. Primus stoves are in wide use through the North. Most stoves used in tents should be vented. There are some nontoxic types. See Chapter 14.

Cooking utensils can be the same as those used on canoe journeys or other camp ventures—the common aluminum nesting pails with wire bails being most suitable. Three of different, average size are ample. A steel frying pan with detachable handle, plates, cups (not aluminum because they become too hot for the lips), knives and forks, bowls, detergent and a brush for washing dishes complete the list of these items. A pair of quart thermos bottles, in a down- or pile-insulated bag, are essential for mug-ups on the winter trail. When harness dogs are used, the driver will need a large pail or kettle about a two-gallon size for cooking dog feed.

Proper, systematic packing of the winter outfit for the trail becomes important. Low temperatures are not conducive to fumbling for items. The midmorning and midafternoon mug-ups should not necessitate the undoing of a large pack on the trail. If the thermos bottles of coffee and the doughnuts are placed in an insulated cloth bag, looped into the lashing ropes of the sled to avoid losing the bag in the snow, the mug-up becomes the easy, pleasant diversion that it should be. The same general packing rules should apply to all remaining items.

Sleeping gear is quickly packed if it is tightly rolled in the tent and tied, the roll to be of such diameter as will fit the sled or toboggan width—usually about fifteen inches.

Since winter travel by dog sled or by the various convey-

The Primus stove

ances described does not require portage-type packs, food is best carried in a light marine plywood grub box with cover, preferably one lined with a thick layer of insulation: cork or Styrofoam. You will recall from Chapter 2 that much of the food taken on a winter wilderness trip is precooked and then frozen into meal-size bricks. To keep these bricks frozen through possible periods of thaw, insulation becomes a necessity. When temperatures drop, the box is kept open for a while to give the contents a deep freezing. The cover is then closed to hold the food through any possible thaw period. (These periods of thaw *can* come. I have seen it rain in the Far North in January, rare as this is.) A second insulated box should be provided to hold food items not requiring a systematic freeze, this insulation then inversely keeping the food items thawed for quicker use. The second box is left open in a heated tent, or near an outdoor open fire, and kept closed whenever it is exposed to the cold. The two-box system prevents much needless thawing and freezing of foods.

Grub boxes are handy on a toboggan since they can form the lower stratum of the sled load, getting other items up away from the snow and brush that rub the lower part of the load. These boxes should be made in a width and length to correspond with the toboggan or sled used. Also, they can be used to form a flat table service—always a luxury in the wilderness.

Extra socks and underwear, together with other miscellaneous items of equipment, go into a packsack. Smaller cloth, drawstring bags within the packsack, separating items into proper categories, make for convenience and avoid confusion of detail.

In packing up, lay the middle of the tent ground cloth across the sled or toboggan, and load on it. If boxes or chests are used for the lower stratum of the load, lay the ground cloth on top of the boxes. Then bring up each side of the ground cloth and lap it across the load. Start the lashing by first fastening one end of the rope to a forward part of the side ropes on a toboggan, or to the front crossbar on a komatik type of sled. Bring the rope across the load and back at a slight angle to the toboggan side rope or a sled crossbar on the opposite side. Continue this crisscross until the rear part of the sled or toboggan is reached, then go back in the same fashion, crossing the original ropes until the front is reached again. The rope should, correctly, describe a series of diamond shapes across the load.

If upstands, also called handlebars, are to be used on the toboggan, the bent-sapling type can be tied in with necessary hitches as the lashing rope reaches these upstands. Carriole or basket-type sleds, of course, are easier to pack.

Cameras need to be carried on the person or in a leather case well secured, high on the load. The momentary picture may otherwise slip from opportunity's grasp. Cameras for sub-zero temperatures need to be sent to the factory for removal of oil, or the intense cold can jam the shutter. This factory service is an expensive procedure, but I cannot suggest a budget shortcut to avoid it. Some expeditions utilize oil-free cameras for winter and other cameras oiled for mild temperatures. This dual-camera system seems to pay off best in the long run if winter travel is annual and the budget permits. An oil resistant to cold is now being developed that seems to promise a solution. Cameras can be carried in an insulated bag, its warmth furnished by the patent hand warmers sold in sporting goods stores. Some winter voyagers carry their cameras under the parka, suspended from a shoulder strap. This provides enough warmth for the camera. (Remember that condensation forms on cameras, guns, etc., when brought from cold to warm temperatures, not from warm to cold.)

Snowshoe types get to be controversial. In recent years snowshoe selection has been largely reduced to a choice between the long, narrow shoe in the proportion of 9″ x 49″, 10″ x 50″, etc., and the wider shoe in the proportion of 12″ x 45″, 13″ x 48″, etc.—both types turned up at the toe. The long, narrow shoe reached a somewhat popular phase because beginning snowshoers are inclined to believe that narrower snowshoes are less apt to interfere with each other in the step. Once it is known that a snowshoe of the 12″ x 45″ or 13″ x 48″ shape does not cause such interference—one shoe passing over the other in the normal walking step—the switchover is generally made to the larger, better-utility shoe.

Proper snowshoe size is based on the weight of the particular wearer. Women, girls, and boys with a weight of about 110 pounds or so should have a shoe 11″ x 42″. An average man of 170 pounds will use a shoe from 12″ x 45″ to 13″ x 48″, heavier men 14″ x 48″ or 50″.

Size of snowshoe relative to weight of wearer is apt to be altered by circumstance. For example, snowshoes used in the Barrens, where packed snow almost supports a man on foot without snowshoes, can be much smaller if all travel is in this region. But the condition can vary from long-packed snow to a fresh fall of soft snow, and from packed snow in open country to softer snow in the scrub forest of the Barrens. Where travel overlaps in these regions, and snow conditions might vary, it is more practical to get a shoe size that will serve—even with some concession—all snow conditions.

Indians in the deep forest sometimes use a very large special hunting snowshoe, much too large for general use. The shoe is used for running down a big game animal that in deep soft snow will be slowed down enough to bring it within rifle shot.

Earlier in the century, types of snowshoes to some extent could point up various Indian cultures and designate geographical tribal locations. This is becoming less so as increased modern transportation facilities are now more available to na-

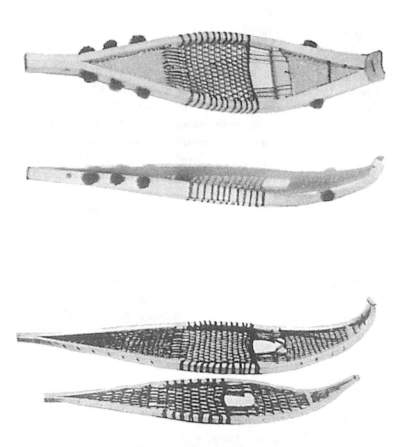

Genuine Indian-made snowshoes from Ogoki
and Oxford House districts—Canada

tives, weaving a shuttle of overlapping culture across the continental wilderness. However, some distinction does still remain. The Naskopi, Beaver Tail, Montagnais, and Tête de Boule, all very wide snowshoes, are some of the earlier, isolated types, now more conspicuously seen in museums, but their relevancy is not forgotten. Perhaps the most striking difference is between the Cree snowshoe and the Ojibway snowshoe, shown in the accompanying illustrations. The Ojibway snowshoe frames are generally made of one piece, having two crossbars; the Cree snowshoe frames with two pieces in the frames and

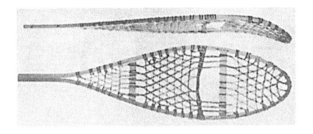

Ojibway or Michigan snowshoe pattern

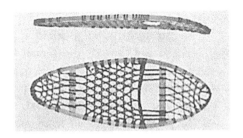

Bear Paw snowshoe

two crossbars. Both are turned up at the toe to prevent the nose of the snowshoe from "diving" under sticks and the down timber which is buried unseen in the snow. It is the one-piece Ojibway that has formed the pattern for most commercial snowshoes made with ash wood frames and cowhide fillers. In the United States this snowshoe is most generally referred to as the Michigan pattern. You will notice that the turned-up toe of the Cree snowshoe is fluted or channeled, giving it a special beauty. Some of the Cree snowshoes are made without the fluted or channel toe, but this seems to be the white man's degrading industrial influence of late years, where high production dominated by white traders outweighed tradition, culture, beauty, and increased practicability. The Bear Paw snowshoe shown in the accompanying illustration is a handy snowshoe around a cabin or for a trapper where a great deal

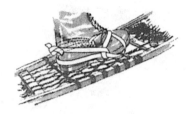

Squaw Hitch snowshoe lashing

of turning and maneuvering is necessary in performing chores. It is not a good general-purpose shoe.

Birch seems to be the most popular wood for snowshoes made by natives, since it can be bent quite well when green, and dries to a hard, strong frame. Also, birch trees are well distributed in much snowshoe country. One objection, sometimes voiced by purists, to factory-produced, commercial snowshoes is that the frames are sawed from planks, risking the possibility of a cross grain that will break in the field. This, I have found, is largely caprice, since snowshoe makers usually are careful to select straight-grained wood. Most native-made snowshoe frames appear slightly irregular, because the wood is split with the grain, not sawed—again, to avoid any possible cross grain. Anyone desiring to make his own snowshoes can do so by soaking the green wood for the frames in a solution of hot water and sal soda to get the wood flexible enough to bend into a snowshoe shape. White ash is a much preferred wood, although birch, hard maple, and many others will make good snowshoes. Hides for the filler are used raw, untanned. They are first dried and cut into strips. The strips are then soaked and laced while slightly damp into the snowshoe frames, the mesh tightening up when completely dry. The shoe is then spar-varnished, giving an attractive, translucent amber effect to the mesh.

Commercial snowshoes are laced most commonly with cowhide. This is a better snowshoe filler than traditionalists will

Semi-sandal-type snowshoe lashing (author's own pattern)

admit. Cowhide, when wet, will stretch, but so will the native-used hides, such as caribou, moose, and deer—the caribou being the best of these. Beaver is still better, but the commercial value of a beaver skin, when prime, prohibits its use, and the restrictions on the trapping of un-prime hides generally excludes its use as a snowshoe filler.

If snowshoe types bring on mild controversy, choice of snowshoe lashings or harness bring on heated arguments. Some will swear by the so-called "Squaw Hitch," shown in the sketch. It is made with lamp wicking, sold by the yard in stores of the North. It is quite popular with Indians. I prefer my own semi-sandal type, with no sole on the sandals in order to prevent snow balling up underneath the foot. The moccasined foot thus bears directly on the snowshoe mesh. The upper heel part of the leather sandal is soaked with spar varnish to make it stiff, the front or toe part of the sandal left soft. To attach, one simply places the toe in the sandal and lowers the heel into the stiffened heel portion. Friction keeps the foot secured, and in the event of a break through ice, the snowshoes can be kicked off. Fur, duffel, or pile can be sewn to the outside of the sandal to add foot warmth. (Also see commercial hitch photo on p. 188.)

Splicing the wood frame of a broken snowshoe is difficult even for a woods craftsman. A small amount of dry raw lacing should be carried for this purpose. The spare lacing and the broken snowshoe are soaked in water, the simplest way being

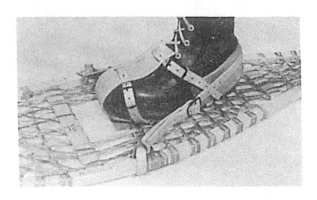

Commercial type snowshoe lashing or binding

under the ice. A splice, if needed, is then made with a piece of hard wood fitted across the break and wrapped with rawhide. As the repaired snowshoe dries, the hide shrinks, forming a tight bond for the mend. The soaking will cause the webbing to sag but when dried will again tighten up. Do not dry the mend rapidly near a stove or open fire, as the mesh will cook.

A field thermometer is an important piece of equipment. It is made to insert into a metal tube or is supported in a cutaway tube to prevent breakage. A daily record of temperatures aids in knowing when to travel, adds to the general winter program, and becomes an interesting post-trip reference.

A wristwatch, because of metal against the skin and a slight circulation restriction of the band, should not be worn in sub-zero temperatures. Rather place the wristwatch in a button flap pocket. If vision glasses are needed on the trail, any metal parts touching the face or head should be covered with wool material, chamois skin, or Indian-tanned fawn skin. Dark glasses need to be worn for protection against snow blindness. This is important all winter, but is more urgent toward the late part of the winter when the sun's declination becomes high. Snow blindness is an inflammation of the eyes, corrected only by days of remaining in the dark. If one of a party does suffer from snow blindness, travel can continue if he is blind-

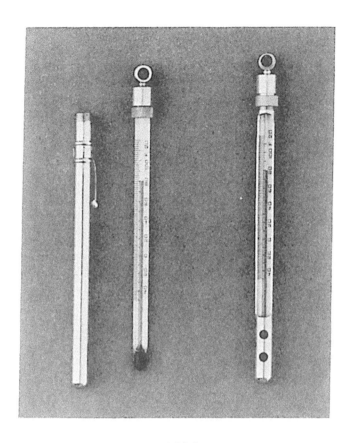

Two types of field thermometers

folded and assumes a position at the upstands or handlebars of the sled or toboggan, to guide him over all smooth travel areas, such as lakes, rivers, etc. Cloudy skies reflect more light than seems apparent, so wear snow glasses when there is any doubt. Green-tinted glass seems to be the most satisfactory. Fasten all glasses around the head with a cord or thong. If snow glasses are lost or broken, use the Eskimo method of carving a pair from wood with horizontal slits instead of lenses. You can improve these by carving both vertical and horizontal slits in the pattern of a plus sign or a "T". The addition of the vertical slit will prevent stumbling over objects not always seen through the horizontal slit. In extreme survival emergency, where it is not possible to carve a wooden pair of sun "glasses," tie two ordinary sticks of wood together and peer out through the uneven cracks left between them.

13

THE WINTER TRIP IN PROSPECT AND PLANNING

ONCE we have decided on the country in which we are to travel, transportation methods become the primary consideration. The wide choice of methods has already been given in Chapter 11. The simplest choice for an average recreation trip is to haul a lightweight but practical camp outfit on a hand-drawn toboggan. This may sound like a grueling task, but it is seldom so. I have pulled a loaded toboggan for days across frozen wilderness lakes and portages with scarcely a tugging reminder, on the lake areas, at least, that it was sliding along behind me. Its sliding surface should, of course, be smooth-sanded and waxed.

There *can* be hard going between lakes, on steep slopes, or on the sea over pack ice. You might need ready hands, strong arms, and muscular legs to hurdle these barriers; even an ax might be needed on the sea ice at times to chop out a trail. Yet, on the whole, mobility in winter on average wilderness travel calls for less physical effort than we exert on a canoe trip with paddle and portage. We can bear in mind for comparison that unlike canoe travel, no pack loads, except with rare exception over a steep rise or snowless stretches of the Barrens, need to be carried on the back. Snow packs hard on lakes, barrens, and sea ice. In the forest, on the other hand, snow piles up deep and light as down. Portage trails will then call for the breaking of a toboggan trail with snowshoes. Snowshoes are needed on the lakes at times too, because packed snow often has a surface crust not quite strong enough to support one's body on foot, and a fresh fall of snow can also impede easy going until such times as it becomes packed by the wind. Yet, these become interesting variables and not insurmountable obstacles.

Winter wilderness trips should be taken well after the solid, initial freeze-up, before too much snow has accumulated through the winter. In the arctic, on the other hand, snow accumulation is generally no problem, and such trips should be taken late in winter after ample snow accumulates. A lack of snow is possible sometimes even in late winter on some snow-blown areas of the arctic. The kind of freeze-up and the degree of latitude naturally will have much to do with the departure time of year. Low temperatures and little or no snow at the beginning of winter allow ice to form fast. As mentioned earlier, the thinner the ice, the faster it thickens, which tends to give safe bearing for travel rather early if temperatures drop abruptly.

Whenever crossing lakes alone, or where there is any doubt as to ice thickness, one should *always carry a light, slim pole* about seven feet long, and keep thumping the end on the ice just ahead at every step. If the ice will hold the thumped pole, it will hold a man. Two inches of good blue ice, it is commonly said, will hold a team of horses, but I don't suggest risking the team or any other comparable weight on this basis. If you should break through when walking over ice and you have a pole for safety, it will span the hole to give you the needed

"A three-man party for a man-hauled toboggan or sled trip has the greatest safety factor."

booster grip for getting back on the ice.

Whenever there is movement of water under ice, however slow, and whatever the general thickness of the ice happens to be, the area above and around the moving water can be a hazard. Any such questionable places should be bypassed on shore where possible. Narrows between bodies of water are likely hazards. While not always apparent, most water moves down a watershed—even that in lake chains, though with varying speed and unpredictable ice-eroding peculiarities.

When hauling a toboggan with more than one man in the party, each will be at the end of a long individual trace, unless one man happens to be at the upstands guiding the toboggan.

If the lead man on a trace should break through the ice, he can be pulled out on the ice by another member of the party. However, the lead man should never wholly rely on only his trace safeguard. He should test any doubtful ice by thumping with a pole. When rescuing somebody, in order to increase good footing purchase on smooth ice, tip the toboggan or sled on its side and quickly tie your trace to the middle of the toboggan, then hang onto this toboggan-moored rope while making the rescue. Most lake ice is covered with snow, which offers considerable resistance to an overturned toboggan or sled.

If a member of the party should break through the ice some distance from shore—usually the least likely place for this to happen—the procedure is to roll out a sleeping bag, strip off the rapidly freezing, wet garments from the victim, and get him, naked, into the sleeping bag. Have a second member of the party go ashore and start a fire. When the fire is going well, unload the toboggan, and haul the victim in the sleeping bag to the fire. Build a big fire, dry out the wet clothes, have a mug-up of coffee, tea, or cocoa and some food, repack and get under way again if the time of day will possibly permit. There is nothing quite so valuable as exercise to reestablish body warmth. The chances of a bad physical reaction from exposure is then slight, and just as important, immediate resumption of travel helps the psychological reaction of the victim. It tends to dispel any mounting apprehensions for later safety.

If the breakthrough is in the nonwooded Barrens, the tent, of course, should be pitched and the stove lighted as soon as possible. Where a break through the ice occurs in a forest region and no equipment such as a sleeping bag is at hand, quickly cover the victim in his wet clothes to the shoulders with snow to prevent the clothes from freezing and to absorb the water. Snow is a powerful absorbent. Build a large fire, undress the victim, wring out his clothes, heat them, then have him don the clothes again and dry them on his body. Exercise around the fire will help to maintain additional body heat. Never thaw or rub frozen parts with snow.

You *can* go alone. Trappers are doing it routinely. There is some risk—but if you keep your wits about you, a great deal less risk, I am sure, than is imagined. Alone, a profound, mysterious peace will be yours—the silence broken only by the rhythmic crunch of your snowshoes, and the occasional basso rumble of the expanding ice beneath your feet. You will hear little elves following your trail. Stop to look back, and they are gone, start and there they are again—elusive little rascals, but friendly. You are not getting "bushy." Actually, what you have been hearing is a secondary swishing sound from your snowshoes—as wisps of ice-granule snow are tossed off at each step. The long, narrow, Indian toboggan is the logical hand-drawn unit for the lone traveler.

For maximum safety on a winter wilderness journey, let your party be three. Find a congenial companion and head into an area where you will have an Indian or Eskimo dog driver with a dog team or power toboggan. He, as the third member of your party, will be a valuable asset to your whole wilderness experience. This triple combination usually works quite well. If something should happen to one member, the other two can usually handle almost any situation. A bad case of illness or injury can be flown out, so it is better that the driver, traveling light and alone making bivouac camps, fetch a plane, while a camp is maintained for the ill or injured member. Even an injured or sick member often can hobble or crawl about and be of some help to himself, unless his condition is too serious.

It is well to point out at this time that many Indians and Eskimos are on the trap line in winter and may not be available as guides. However, one usually can make arrangements well ahead of the trip on a basis that will offer attractive alternative pay to trapping.

A three-man party for a man-hauled toboggan or sled trip

has the greatest safety factor. The addition of the third man reduces the pack load proportionately for two. The third man, moreover, adds to mobility and cuts down on encampment labor. Two men pulling, well spaced on long traces, a third guiding the load over rough places with the upstands, alternating these positions among the three men for relief, is good routine procedure. There are times when one man pulling, one at the upstands, another on a gee pole will manage a load over a stretch of rather bad going, such as pack ice or rough, abruptly inclined portage trails. A gee pole can be cut in the forest, the required hole in one end drilled with a pocketknife, the pole then fastened through this hole to the forepart of the toboggan with rawhide. Pushing sidewise or ahead with the gee pole, depending on the circumstance, can give great lateral control together with a hauling advantage over these rough areas.

Rather long lengths of No. 5 sash cord, or its nylon equivalent, from thirty to fifty feet, are used for the traces when the toboggan is man-pulled; No. 6 to 8 sash cord when pulled by dogs or a motorized unit.

Head straps similar to those used on packsacks, or tumplines, attached to the long rope traces, are needed for the haulers. The head straps used in various hauling positions give relief: across the forepart of the head, diagonally across the chest from shoulder to underarm, or across the waist. Heavy canvas is best for these head straps. Ordinary commercial leather becomes stiff and cold. Heavy, smoke-tanned moosehide is very good.

Some prefer a regular hauling harness—two canvas straps passing over the shoulders and under the arms to the trace directly behind. I think, however, that you will like the variable positions of the head strap method better.

Where a winter trail is chosen along a summer canoe route, most of the travel except the summer portages is across frozen lakes and on river ice. Along coasts, travel is also on ice trails, but here pack ice or some salient land point extending into the sea sometimes requires detours inland that serve as shortcuts. Also, now and then, there are specially cut winter trails for shortening routes.

Under ordinary conditions the load moves along over ice with comparative ease. Of course, different temperatures make the ease of sledding vary. Higher temperatures make easier going. The process is not usually one, as some believe, of tugging away like a team of draft horses pulling a plow, but rather a leisurely stride and light pull, where conversation can be carried on in a normal voice, even though individuals of the party are separated by long traces. Sound carries well in the cold, crisp air.

There will be a strong tendency to adopt the motorized toboggan instead of the hand-drawn unit. The objection voiced toward the daylong exhaust sound is understandable, but once in camp, quiet descends again. Also, the speed of the motorized toboggan is such that only a few hours of daylight need be devoted to mechanized travel, leaving the remaining daylight for quiet wilderness diversion. For solitude and the study of winter wildlife, one can make all-day trips away from a fixed base camp on snowshoes without the motorized unit.

Travel security is best maintained with two motorized units in the event of mechanical breakdown. Of course, the trailer toboggan in an emergency can be hand drawn, but an abandoned motorized toboggan can mean a substantial financial loss. Flying it out on the undercarriage of a plane is expensive —about a dollar or so per mile. It can, of course, be towed out later with another motorized toboggan, or repaired with new parts brought in.

A compromise arrangement used by some trappers in rough country is an extremely light, wood-frame sled, consisting of little more than braced runners lashed to a backpack. When the packer carrying the load on his back has hurdled the obstacles insurmountable with a sled, he lays his sled-pack on the frozen lake and pulls it, only to pick it up again for backpacking to hurdle another tough barrier.

Backpacking trips in any kind of country require bold, self-disciplined trimming down and careful selection of equipment. Mountain-packing where the travel contour may be rough to the point of some actual scaling or climbing, the mountain-pack frame or mountain-type packsack will be used. Bulky forest-packing, however, works best with the Duluth packsack —the items in the pack so adjusted as to conform in shape to the packer's back. This requires a contour-packing method best accomplished if the pack is laid face down, the items inserted so as to be bulkier on the sides than in the center of the pack. The pack will then form-fit the back. The pack should have a head strap, sometimes incorrectly referred to as a "tumpline." (A true tumpline is a combination head strap with two eight-foot straps for lashing the pack bundle. See my book, *The New Way of the Wilderness*, published by The Macmillan Company.)

Backpacking immediately suggests that several utility items ordinarily carried on a dog sled, or other conveyance, must be eliminated. The shovel, saw, wood-burning stove, and so on, obviously cannot be included. The two-and-one-half pound, double-bitted ax, well sheathed, must, however, be a part of the backpacking outfit, unless travel is on the Barrens, where a Primus stove is used, and no wood is to be cut. Then the Primus stove and fuel, of course, replace the ax. A small Whelen type of lean-to tent can be used in the forest. A wedge or pyramid tent will replace the lean-to tent on the Barrens, or the lean-to tent must be closed with a front, drop-type canopy to hold in the heat of the Primus stove.

For backpacking, sleeping units will be reduced to the common mummy type of sleeping bag, or to the half-bag previously described, in order to reduce weight. Cooking utensils need to be as light as possible—two pails of smaller size being ample for one or two men.

Foods for backpacking must of necessity be water-free to drastically cut down weight. Backpacking in winter should not be considered unless the terrain is too rough for a toboggan or travel is on the Barrens at a time when heavily windblown areas are apt to become free from snow.

You will have to evaluate your own transportation methods. If you are one who loves solitude and the mysterious grandeur of the winter wilderness, your choice will not be easy. Will you settle for the peace and quiet of the winter night even though the day be shattered by the continuous, raucous exhaust of a motorized toboggan? Does hauling a toboggan by hand seem too much of an ordeal for the reward of a silent and enchant-ing wilderness throughout the journey? If neither of these merits your consideration, then seek out that Indian or Eskimo with the dog team.

Would you like to see the winter wilderness on less tradi-tional terms? Then, if your budget will allow, charter a flight with one of the various companies who carry on the business of flying to Hudson's Bay outposts. I scarcely need remind you however, that chartered flights are expensive. Plan chartered flights on the basis of a dollar per mile with small planes of the Cessna type. Double the cost for heavier planes such as the Norseman or Beaver. Rates are based on double mileage. In other words, a 300 mile flight at a dollar per mile would be $300, though the plane travels 600 miles on its round trip. Flights are sometimes scheduled between Posts, which greatly reduces the cost.

Hudson's Bay Posts generally furnish meals and lodging at a specified rate. You can make all-day trips by dog sled from such Posts and even return to them in time for the evening meal. Or, you can use your man-hauled toboggan and equip-ment for trips out from the Post, camping out as many nights as you wish, and returning to the Post. Many of these Posts are remotely located, so that a day's travel from them on snow-shoes will have you well into wilderness areas.

If you desire periodic change in the kind of country from forest to barrens, to mountains, to coastal regions, you can charter flights or avail yourself of scheduled flights, and move on. Many of the Posts now have two-way radio communication, so that you can make these periodic reservations well ahead. Your camp outfit, including a hand-drawn toboggan, can readily be carried in a plane. If time and budget permit, you can cover a large part of the North American continent in this fashion. Scheduled flights will cost a great deal less, but they are not always available. Sometimes these "scheduled" flights are based on the current accumulation of a pay load, and do not depart regularly. Always make inquiries well ahead. Or, if you have the leisure and temperament of a true voyageur—just bide your time and move fortuitously on. It can pay great dividends of adventure.

Long motorized toboggan trips, where daily camps are pitched, can be so planned as to reach Hudson's Bay Posts for provisioning, refueling, overnight stops, and the interest such diversion offers. Some Posts are at wilderness settlements, and include a Royal Canadian Mounted Police Post, a mission, and an Indian agency. Even though stops are planned nightly at Hudson's Bay Posts, camp equipment should be carried in the event of breakdown.

With some hesitancy I will touch on a subject that is often posed to me where winter activity is concerned. What about alcoholic beverages "to warm the body and spirit"? I have found through longtime observation that you are a lot better off with hot coffee, tea, or cocoa.

A half century of watching sub-zero temperatures mixed with alcohol shows that the man who drinks in the winter wilderness runs about the same risk as the man who drinks and drives a car. When an ample amount of "grog" is in the pack, there is a temptation in low temperatures to overindulge. Carelessness may ensue, and with cold weather, most often does. The final result can be amputation of a frozen hand, a foot, face surgery, and so on. Now and then, a frozen body is flown out for burial.

Scientific data on alcohol as it affects the body at low temperatures is lengthy and technical but comes out about as follows: Even when not overindulging, a drink of alcoholic liquor in sub-zero weather gives not warmth to the body but a false feeling of allaying the cold. Actually, it acts as an anesthetic, not a stimulant, lowering sensibility and resistance to cold. Here lies the danger. A part of the body is apt to freeze without one being aware of it. When the effects of alcohol wear off, the body has also suffered a degree of functional setback, so that it does not resist the cold quite to the extent that it did before each successive drink. That is, drinking results in a sort of progressive deterioration of one's resistance to cold. And with this much said, I leave the matter of grog on the winter trail to your own personal discretion and wisdom.

Smoking also reduces one's resistance to cold. Nicotine is a vasoconstrictor. That is, it cuts down (constricts) the flow of blood through the blood vessels, causing the extremities to become cold and risking frostbite.

CHAPTER

14

THE PORTABLE
WINTER CAMP

A COMMON misconception that winter camping and travel is an
ordeal practiced only by hardy individuals with low sensibility
to pain and cold should be discarded with other current wilderness fallacies. However, the belief that a sleeping bag can
be rolled out on the snow in the open at any temperature for
comfortable sleep is also an illusion. Why anyone should un-
necessarily resort to corporal punishment for sheer bravado, I
have never been able to grasp. A tent properly pitched in a
winter wilderness, equipped with a heating unit, allows comfortable sleeping, eating, dressing, reading, or any other function at sub-zero temperatures. If the camp is to be a bivouac in
the forest, the matter of comfort rests on a lean-to, an open
fire, a backlog, and proper sleeping gear.

In any of these instances, no foolhardy stunts are performed.
In a tent camp the heat generated from wood or liquid fuel is
confined by the enclosed tent. In a bivouac the fire is built

large and in the open—heat for cooking, warmth, drying, leisure, and other diversion being supplied by systematically controlled reflection and convection.

This same general heating principle used in the bivouac camp, applies when any open front tent or lean-to in various modifications is used—an open fire and a backlog.

Whatever the country traveled and the type of camp used, there are appropriate methods to follow. We can thus overrule the bravado approach, and the opposite extreme—the needless apprehension that winter camping must inevitably be an ordeal. Some deviation from the above routine camping methods is unavoidable in actual mountain-peak-scaling night stops. (Scaling mountain peaks is a specialized pursuit requiring individual treatment.) In this volume we are primarily concerned with general winter wilderness camping techniques and travel in forest, on the Barrens, sea ice, prairie, and traversable mountain trails.

The forest camp, using tent and stove or lean-to and open fire, is best made deep in the protection of a grove whenever possible. Protection against wind adds greatly to warmth and to reduced fuel needs. Grove protection might erroneously suggest that the camp could also be made in the lee of a hill, or under the protection of a cliff. This, we need to emphasize, can be hazardous, for snow will drift deeply into leeward places. Occupants of tents have been victims of monoxide poisoning while using unvented gas units or where heavy drifting covered the tent and blocked the venting of the heating units themselves. Icing of tents due to sleet can also prevent air from reaching sleepers through the porousness of tent fabric, where no vents are used with Primus stoves. A deep forest grove, however, is not likely to create drifting hazards over properly vented tents.

As one pulls into a selected camping place in a forest grove, snow needs to be shoveled away not only to provide tent space but to clear the area around the tent for general freedom of movement. Snow should not, however, be cleaned down to the ground under the sleeping area. About six inches of snow should be left for insulation. Shoveling finished, a number of small balsam or spruce trees are cut and carried intact to the camp spot for use as tent poles. The lopped-off boughs are used for covering the sleeping area.

Judgment needs to be exercised in the cutting of such trees. Advantageous thinning can be done—always keeping in mind the betterment of forest growth rather than its destruction, even though its remoteness at times seems to make the cutting of little consequence.

A snowshoe will do as a makeshift snow shovel for clearing the camp area, but at best it is inefficient. I have found that the light aluminum scoop shovel is well worth carrying where transportation is by dogs or motorized toboggan, and you might not find its weight prohibitive on a hand-pulled toboggan. A short, very broad-bladed canoe paddle, the blade end sawed square, will serve better as a snow shovel than a snowshoe, but is much less efficient than an aluminum scoop shovel. The paddle is, of course, light in weight and easily stowed on a toboggan.

After much experiment I find the wedge tent, 7′ x 9′ for two men, and 8′ x 10′ for three men, about right. The tent should be made of a tight-weave, high-count, waterproofed, fire-resisting, cotton tent material, and should be of the double-tent type for greatest comfort—a space of about one and one half inches provided between the inside and outside tent. Light tapes for tying the double tents together into the spaced position with each other are provided at the ridge, base, and the intermediate positions along the tent slopes. The inside tent is then disregarded in the pitching process, the outside tent when pitched having the function of positioning both tents without an individual adjustment of the inner tent, except for the straightening out of sod cloths.

Twelve-inch-wide sod cloths must be provided on both inside and outside tents. The sod cloths of the outside tent are to be drawn out from the outside tent, the inside tent sod cloths drawn in from the inside. In a forest camp some of the balsam or spruce boughs are laid on top of the sod cloths, some underneath. This prevents the sod cloths from freezing to the snow. Since stakes cannot be driven in winter, poles cut in the forest are laid on the boughs on the outside sod cloths, the poles extending well beyond the tent. Boughs are then laid generously on the extended ends of the poles and snow shoveled over the boughs and sod cloths to hold down the tent.

By this method the tent snugly seals its occupants from the cold. The only remaining jobs, once the tent base is set, are to raise the ridge of the tent with poles and guy out the poles with the ridge rope, then install the heating unit. If trees are conveniently located, no poles are needed, the ridge rope then going directly to the trees. When poles are used to hold up the tent, the ridge rope is brought from tent to poles and down to a "deadman," and there tied. (A deadman in this instance is a pole that has been covered with boughs and buried in the snow.) The tent ridge rope has been passed around the center of the deadman pole before burying, of course, the loose end of the rope left out on top of the snow where it is accessible and can be drawn up tight to adjust the tent. This loose end is then brought back from around the deadman to anywhere along the taut part of the ridge rope, and there secured with a taut-line hitch. The taut-line hitch is extremely valuable because it permits variable adjustment of the ridge rope without having to untie it. Note that the ridge rope has been attached to the tent-supporting pole with a clove hitch. This type of hitch also permits variable adjustment, since it can be raised or lowered, and even allows the tent pole to be moved in and out as needed to give perfect wrinkle-free stretch to the tent. Parrel ropes attached to tent walls for holding walls out full can also be tied with adjustable taut-line hitch to bushes or trees nearby. (See illustration of taut-line and clove hitches on p. 206.)

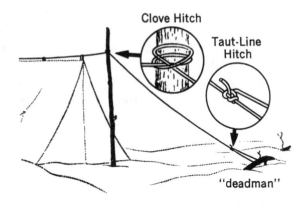

Taut-line hitch and clove hitch showing practical application

The following is a simple, easily adapted principle for obtaining a perfect rectangle of the tent at the base and keeping the walls smooth. When about to pitch the tent, first tie the entrance flaps shut. Then spread out the base of the tent in its approximate intended position. Draw the rear end of the tent out taut and fasten it down as described, using poles, boughs, and snow. Grab the front corners of the tent and bring them together to a point and draw them out taut. You will so far have formed a triangle with the bottom edge of the tent. When this triangle is brought out taut, the front point of the triangle assumes a definite point that cannot be moved in any direction unless it is given slack. This point determines the exact center of the tent at the front. By using a stick or ax handle, measure over half the width of the tent from this front center point to both sides and fasten down the walls as described earlier. You will find when you now raise the tent that it will assume a perfect rectangle and be free from wrinkles. (If the tent has previously been badly pitched and pulled out of shape, it may have wrinkles when using the above principle. However, by using the principle described, the tent will eventually be

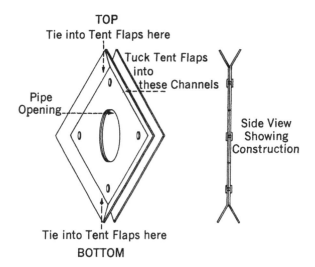

TOP
Tie into Tent Flaps here

Tuck Tent Flaps into these Channels

Pipe Opening

Side View Showing Construction

Tie into Tent Flaps here
BOTTOM

Pipe thimble

stretched back into proper shape—especially after a few melting-snow wettings.)

Next in order is to set up the wood- or oil-burning stove. The pipes will be of short lengths, or telescopic, stored in the stove for convenient transportation. Set the stove near the exit, just far enough from the tent flaps to avoid their scorching. These front flaps should be styled to run open all the way to the ridge, *not* partway as most wedge tents are made. The overlap of the tent flaps should be generous and tied shut with cords or tapes. Avoid zippers if you value peace of mind. About a foot from the ridge between the flaps, tie in the pipe thimble. The thimble is made of two sheets of aluminum riveted together, with the edges of both aluminum sheets flared out as shown in the accompanying illustration. The pipe will be of four-inch diameter for wood, three-inch for oil.

The vent pipe can be run straight up through a thimble in the roof of the tent, but this incurs a risk of sparks falling down on the tent and burning holes, or setting the tent afire. Projecting the pipe through the tent flaps is much safer, although it entails a little additional pipe. Another objection to the pipe going straight up is that a snowfall causes melting snow water to run down the pipe onto the stove, with a continual sleep-disturbing hiss, smell, and soon a badly rusted stove and iron-oxide mess. Whether you choose to have the pipe go out between the tent flaps or out of the tent roof, it should have a T at the end of the pipe opening to prevent snow-block. If the pipe is brought through the roof, the tent material should be so treated that when a spark does burn a hole, the burning will not spread. Tent makers supply waterproofing, spark-resisting compounds, or materials so treated.

When burning wood a backdraft damper needs to be installed in the pipe near the stove, so that the stove may be fully filled with wood before retiring and the fire kept properly dampered all night. With the backdraft damper open, draft air goes directly into the vent pipe and not through the fuel in the stove. A slow fire will then continue to burn all night because it has the least possible air for combustion, yet the fire is not smothered. In the morning all that one needs to do is close the backdraft, open the regular draft which supplies air directly to the fuel, add more wood, and crawl back into bed. In a few moments the tent is warm. There should also be another damper within the vent pipe for additional control to help radiate the heat and keep it from going up the chimney when the fire is going well. If this explanation of the backdraft principle is given to a tinsmith, he will know from daily practice in his line exactly what to supply without further information.

A very good stove for the tent sizes given is the smallest, flat, oval-top, top-feeding, black, sheet metal stove, known currently in hardware stores as an "airtight." Food is handily cooked on its flat top surface.

The United States Army developed an excellent unit for burning almost any kind of liquid fuel along with solid fuels, in the traditional "Yukon" stove. (The Yukon stove is simply a rectangular sheet metal stove that has a front gate opening for feeding it with wood, and has a common vent pipe.) To this stove, the Army has applied a simple gravity-feed burner for liquid fuel, set in a round opening cut into the top surface of the stove. Since the liquid fuel burner does not extend more than an inch or less into the stove, both liquid fuel and wood can be burned at the same time—or either one alone—thereby reducing the consumption of liquid fuel. Wood when burned with liquid fuel can be either dry or green, the green wood being consumed by the added combustion of the liquid fuel. Thus, on the tundra, such fuel as green or dry willow shrub can help to amplify the liquid gasoline or kerosene fuel supply. Air for the liquid fuel is supplied from the common draft created by the vent pipe. The Army unit, complete with Yukon stove, burner, vent pipe, and spark arrestor, is now sold in surplus.

The Army burner supplied with the Yukon stove for burning liquid fuel can be adapted to the airtight. If this item should be exhausted in surplus supply, the burner being very simple in construction may be commercially made up for one's individual use.

The so-called "safety" heaters operating on a catalytic principle have been the focus of much interest as tent heaters, because of their non-vent, non-toxic principle. Two of these are shown in the illustrations on pp. 210 and 211. Platinum forms the catalyst to combine the liquid fuel vapors with oxygen to generate the heat. Naphtha gas, generically, is the fuel used, although comparable naphtha products are sold under patent names, usually in sealed gallon cans which can be disposed of as the fuel is used up. Because this type of heating unit has to be started on vaporized gas fuel and not on liquid gas that later vaporizes from heat, a problem is encountered in temperatures below minus 15 degrees Fahrenheit. Below this temperature the unit needs to be warmed up before it will vaporize the gas in its tank, and the tank must also be insulated from the cold to maintain its warmth. Alcohol is used to prime the unit, and at severe temperatures, the unit may

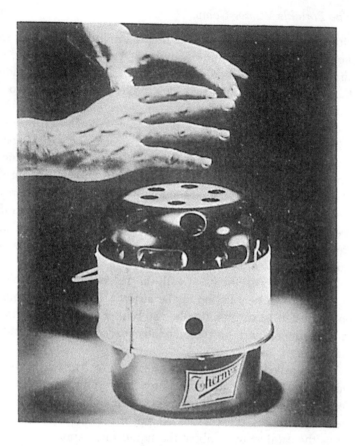

Catalytic-type heater
(*minimum 3,000 BTU output*), *Model 30*

have to be primed three or four times.

The pre-warming or multiple priming is not practical in the mobile camp on the tundra. But since the catalytic heater is noiseless and has a great safety advantage as a night heater in a tent when the party is asleep, needing no vent, its use might well be considered in conjunction with another type of heater in which liquid gas can be burned at the start, if the transportation method used will allow the weight of this extra unit.

Catalytic-type heater
(minimum 4,000 BTU output), Model 57C

Then, for cooking and heating while the party is active in camp, the unit burning liquid gas at the start can be used, the catalytic heater meantime being warmed for use when the party is asleep. In the tent sizes given, the Model 57C will cut back the severe temperature just enough to give comfort when the party are in their winter type sleeping bags. A gallon of naphtha gas will last about three nights, or about thirty hours, in this model—a gas economy feature which warrants the extra weight of the catalytic heater for the sleeping period.

The arctic pyramid tent has been a successful unit for the Barrens and sea ice by virtue of its unique pitching principle and double-walled design. Tent poles are of one-piece aluminum and are permanently attached to the outside corner ridges

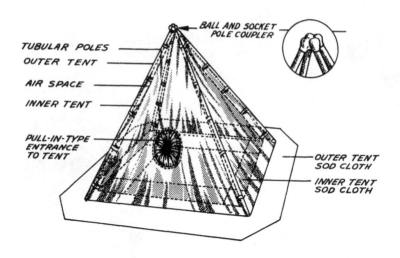

BALL AND SOCKET
POLE COUPLER

TUBULAR POLES

OUTER TENT

AIR SPACE

INNER TENT

PULL-IN-TYPE
ENTRANCE
TO TENT

OUTER TENT
SOD CLOTH

INNER TENT
SOD CLOTH

The arctic pyramid tent

of the tent. The pole ends come together in a ball-and-socket assembly at the peak. When decamping, the tent is rolled up with the poles attached and laid lengthwise on the dog sled or motorized toboggan trailer for transporting. On being pitched, the tent is pulled out and set on the ground like a four-legged "tripod" covered with fabric. It is supplied with a floor cloth but can be made with sod cloths and a loose floor cloth if desired. The floor cloth can then also be used for a sled pack cloth, reducing somewhat the load weight.

Once the pyramid tent is set up, camp equipment and provisions are brought inside and set near the wall on the floor cloth or sod cloths, to hold down the tent. A second tent unit is then slipped over the first, much in the fashion that a woman brings a dress down over her head. The poles at the corner ridges hold the second tent about two inches out away from the first tent. Thus, an insulating air space is created between the two tent units. The outside tent must also have a sod cloth on which additional weights are placed to hold it down against the wind. The pyramid shape makes it very resistant to wind,

The bivouac lean-to forest camp

but a light, No. 5 sash cord guy rope from the peak to a dead-man anchor helps on the windward side, if the blow is heavy. This anchor can be made by freezing down a peg with a cup of water, or using a deadman in the snow as previously described, using some camp item, such as an ice chisel, for attaching the rope under the snow. The main weight on the outside sod cloth is the sled, which is tipped on its side and routinely set on the windward sod cloth. The weight of occupants in the tent on the floor or sod cloths, of course, supplies additional anchor load, especially when the occupants are lying down. A vent is supplied in this tent for use with a Primus stove. The entrance is of the pull-in "sock" type for sealing out any possible obtruding drafts. It is then tied shut on the inside.

The arctic pyramid and the wedge tent have proved to be the two basic types most suitable for arctic travel. The wedge tent rather than the pyramid will best be used in forest areas. Both stand winds of the Barrens better than other types. Wall tents are an abomination when pitching problems on frozen ground are involved. Also, their vertical walls offer too much "sail" in heavy blows.

Forest camps with an open fire are of three general types: a reflecting-type open-front tent before a fire, a simple tarp used as a lean-to before a fire, and a bivouac lean-to before a fire—the latter constructed entirely from materials gathered in the immediate forest area. All three general types are used in combination with a backlog erected with logs. A backlog, by its principle of creating a semi-vacuum, serves a dual purpose—not only does it draw the smoke away from the tent, it also reflects the heat forward to the tent or lean-to. A glance at the forest bivouac illustration (p. 213) will show this backlog construction. For the bivouac lean-to, as this same illustration shows, start with a horizontal pole held against two trees by two crotched sticks. Lean additional poles against this horizontal pole, extending them at a good slope down to the ground. Then shingle the sloping poles with evergreen boughs. Now, to create the semi-vacuum mentioned, build the fire between the bivouac lean-to and the backlog, which will then carry off the smoke and reflect the heat back to the lean-to. In the bivouac type, as in all camps, sleeping units are carried as part of the equipment, but the bivouac is sometimes used without sleeping robes in emergency for survival stopovers.

The igloo or snow house is one of the most romantic shelters. Though still in use during hunting trips on the sea ice, its use is diminishing among Eskimos with the advent of heated tents and access to material for cabins. Something should, however, be said about its construction.

Snow blocks laid in simple tiers

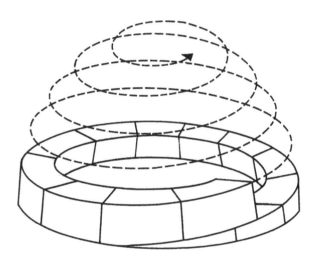

Snow blocks laid on an incline

Two basic methods can be used in the building of an igloo or snow house: one where snow blocks are laid in simple tiers, like bricks; the other where the blocks are laid on an incline to form a continuous spiral to the dome. The second method offers a more secure way for those making a first attempt, because the blocks tie in with little chance of collapse as the construction reaches the most difficult part—the dome.

In the spiral method a thin snow block wedge is cut and laid, followed by blocks each successively a little thicker than the preceding block, until a full round is completed, the last block laid being full size. After this graduated first round of blocks is laid, all blocks will be full size.

It will be apparent that as the second round of blocks and those following are being laid, all blocks will be lying on an uphill course, due to the slope of the first round, and will continue on this uphill course until the snow house is completed. As the spiral goes up, the blocks will be set inward a little to form the dome shape of the igloo. The last three or four blocks do not, of course, come to a neat fit at the dome, but this offers no problem since the irregularity caused by the spiral construction is easily trimmed off with a snow knife. Any voids left by faulty-shaped blocks are readily filled with snow.

Snow houses ice up in time with the prolonged use of Primus stoves and lose their porous ventilating property. Eskimos abandon such iced-up houses and build new ones. A satisfactory innovation exists for safely using these old snow houses. The dome is cut out with a snow knife or ax to a diameter of two or three feet and covered with a simple round canvas cap in which a vent pipe thimble has been inserted. The vent pipe for an oil stove is then slipped through the thimble until the pipe reaches the bead on a pipe joint. Here the bead catches the thimble and pushes up the canvas dome to "peak it" for shedding a snowfall. The canvas rim where it hangs over the snow house wall has loops that serve to stake the canvas to the snow house with aluminum stakes carried for this purpose, or the canvas can be wetted along the rim and lightly frozen to the snow house.

It will be seen that the use of this compromise between a snow house and a tent, using the canvas cap, will also allow the making of a new snow house without having to complete the most difficult part—the dome.

In areas where snow packs solid enough for blocks, regular tents can be made more comfortable by building up only windbreaks around them. These windbreaks should be built in an arc, or horseshoe shape—not square—for strength. The value of snow blocks for these windbreaks and for pitching a tent on the Barrens will be apparent to the reader. Here, the blocks are laid on the outside sod cloth for ballast and for a windbreak.

Snow packs sufficiently for snow house use only where fallen snow is in the open where it can be subjected to high winds. Snow in the forest does not pack.

Snow knives are available in large supply at any army surplus store.

ITEMIZED EQUIPMENT

THE following is designed for a winter wilderness journey of one month for a party of three. The list can be adapted to shorter or longer periods and to size of party by inspection of each item for proportionate additions or deletions, based on wear and consumption, as applied to socks, flashlight batteries, fuel, etc. The personal items are listed for each member of the party, the camping equipment for all three members.

CLOTHING AND PERSONAL ITEMS
FOR ONE INDIVIDUAL

Long underwear, wool	2 drawers, 2 shirts
Undergarments, down	1 suit
Outer shirt, wool, jersey, or sweater, lightweight	1
Duffel socks	4 pairs
Socks, wool, heavy weight	4 pairs
Pants, soft weave, wool, or high-count poplin over down underpants	1 pair
Short pants, pile	1 pair
Belt and suspenders (braces)	1 pair
Parka, down, pile, or fur with ruff	1
Anorak (windbreaker), thin, high-count poplin, with buttons on hood to attach fur ruff	1
Overshoes, lightweight, four-buckle for wet weather	1 pair
Moccasins or mukluks for extremely cold, dry weather	1 pair
Stocking or ski cap, wool	1
Bandanna handkerchief	1
Mittens, moosehide with liners of duffel, pile, down or fur	1 pair
Wristlets, wool	1 pair
Wallet or money belt	1
Watch, pocket type, or carry wristwatch in pocket	1
Compass, cruiser type	1
Waterproof match safe	1

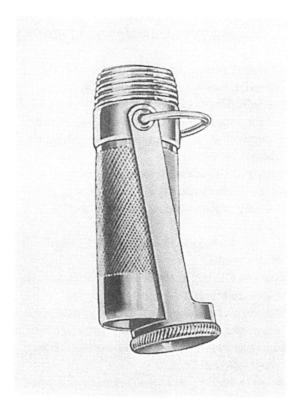

Waterproof match safe

Matches (see Provision List)
Belt knife, five- or six-inch blade, and sheath	1 each
Glasses, if needed for vision	2 pairs
Snow glasses	1 pair
Toilet articles, including hand towel	1 set
Diary and No. 1 (soft) lead pencil (no pens)	1 each
Map of region	1
Binoculars, compact type, 7- or 8-power	1 pair

CAMP EQUIPMENT FOR THREE

Sleeping robe or bag, down or fur, including air mattress or down-insulated cot	3 sets
Hudson's Bay blanket or other type for use over ground cloth and under sleeping units (single blanket covers three-man sleeping area)	1
Packsacks, Duluth or Poirer, No. 2 or 3	2
Provision box (insulated) with cover (cover closed with rawhide laces—not metal hinges)	2
Ax, double-bitted, two-and-one-half pound, with sheaths	1
Saw, Swedish type, thirty-inch; or chain saw (include oil-mixed gas)	1
Whetstone, combination fine and coarse surface, Alundum, for sharpening ax and knife	1
Oil, light, clear type for stone, in leakpoof, army-type field can	1
File for working down nicked ax and sharpening Swede saw	1
Flashlight, with extra bulbs and long-life type mercury batteries	1 set
Lantern, gasoline (optional, but with long nights and some camps pitched after dark, this is a valuable item. Also adds in heating tent)	1
White gasoline, special lantern type	For length of trip
Ice-fishing tackle	1 set
Ice chisel	1

Toboggan or sled, hand-drawn, by dogs, or motorized toboggan (include ropes; see Chapter 11)	1
Dog team or motorized toboggan, including trailer toboggan or sled when using motorized toboggan	1
Dog harness	1 for each dog
Dog moccasins, canvas	6 sets for each dog
Motorized-toboggan repair tools, clutch belts, and extra spark plugs	1 set
Gasoline, oil, and motor-priming compounds for motorized toboggan	For length of trip
Tent, for the Barrens, the arctic pyramid type with ground sheet and aluminum poles; for forest, the wedge type with ground sheet and generous pitching ropes	1
Snow shovel, lightweight, aluminum, scoop type	1
Firearms and ammunition, if permitted (not legal in field of some countries outside hunting season; not necessary for protection; check restrictions of country to be traveled—.22 caliber rifle now allowed off-season in Canada)	
Camera equipment and film	1 set
Primus stove or army outfit described in text, if on the Barrens or open prairie	1
Airtight stove if traveling in forest region, with pipe and tent flap thimble	1
Sewing and repair kit: rawhide thongs for sled and snowshoes; canvas, needles, and thread for dog harness	1 kit

Carpenter's small block plane and piece of
 heavy wool cloth or fur if sled runners are
 to be iced   1 kit
Pocketknife, cattleman's type, with leather
 punch blade for drilling holes in wood and
 leather   1
First-aid items: obtain Red Cross Manual and
 standard Red Cross kit, or consult family
 physician   1 kit
Toilet paper, see Provision List   For length
                  of trip

COOKING UTENSILS FOR THREE

Cooking pails, aluminum, nesting type	3
Bowls, aluminum	3
Cups, stainless steel (not aluminum, too hot for the mouth)	3
Plates, aluminum	3
Spoons	3
Forks	3
For knives, use each individual's sheath knife instead of table knives	3
Frying pan with removable, field-improvised, wood handle; unless on the Barrens, then fixed handle	1
Thermos bottles, standard, or with wide mouth	1 for each member
Can opener (not required unless some canned foods are taken)	1
Aluminum shaker with one foot of plated chain placed inside for quickly mixing dry whole milk	2
Dish towels	2
Dishwashing brush	1
A two-gallon or larger pail for cooking or heating dog food, if dogs are used for transportation	1

ON JOURNEYS WHERE POSITIONS NEED
TO BE DETERMINED BY SPECIAL
INSTRUMENT OBSERVATIONS
(Over and Above the Magnetic Compass)

Light explorer's transit or sextant and artificial horizon	1 set
Radio, small transistor type, combination standard and short wave for navigation time signals, radio lines of position, weather reports, news and amusement; supply with mercury-type batteries	1
Aerial wire, very flexible, standard type for radio when signals are weak; suspend from tent poles, trees, etc.; also, a short piece of wire, one end attached to a four-inch piece of copper rod for a ground where needed; lay rod deep in snow near ground	50 feet
Plotting equipment: Mercator charts, protractor, dividers, pencils	1 set
Nautical Almanac or Solar Ephemeris (Sheets for dates of trip only may be removed to save weight)	1
H.O. 214 Tables for proper range of latitude (issued in volumes of 10 degrees each)	1
Astrocompass (near magnetic pole only)	1
Polarized Sky Compass (in arctic only)	1
For information on route finding and equipment, see my book, *The Wilderness Route Finder,* published by The Macmillan Company, New York City; this book contains a comprehensive, nontechnical treatment of how to find the way through wilderness	

Sextant and artificial horizon

areas of the world, including short celestial
navigation methods that will be understood
by all

The foregoing general list of equipment contains the essentials for a winter trip, where transportation is by hand-drawn
toboggan, dog sled, or motorized toboggan.

It will be obvious that this list will have to be drastically
reduced for a backpacking trip.

Where two or more motorized toboggans and trailers are
used, the load limit may be allowed to rise materially if the
route is not too rough. One can include such items as a chain
saw; a larger, roomier tent, and virtually any other item that
the members of the party desire for more luxurious living. But
here too, excess weight and too wide a variety can be an in-
convenience rather than a luxury.

WINTER FOODS

In preparing a food budget, the method of transportation will obviously determine to a great extent the nature and variety of foods. Where the load will be carried by dog sled or on a trailer behind a motorized toboggan, the already cooked, water-content meat, such as stew, meatballs, or fresh, un-cooked meat, can be carried. Where load limit must be cut for hand-drawn sled or toboggan trips, meats and stews can, if necessary, be of the freeze-dried variety.

All meat for backpacking should be carried as freeze-dried. Bread, doughnuts, and fruitcake will have to be eliminated in favor of carrying a dry patent biscuit mix, if the distance is extensive. Various breads, plain and enriched, can readily be baked in the frying pan as bannock, propped up before an open fire. Hot bread is a wintertime luxury.

With the comparatively short periods of daylight in winter, cooking should be kept to a minimum for convenience. The stews described in Chapter 2 will, of course, be prepared in advance, separated into daily three-men rations and merely heated. The entire food budget will then be resolved into the following:

Stewed meat as described in Chapter 2
Stew can be varied with meatballs in gravy, or baked beans
   —these treated in the same fashion as the stew
Fresh meat—steak, each steak separated and wrapped in
   waxed paper to prevent freeze bonding
Bacon—each slice separated and wrapped in waxed paper
Freeze-dried scrambled eggs
Instant potato
Butter

Dry whole milk (always include chain mixing can described)

Shortening (solid, not liquid type) for frying meat—or use accumulated bacon fat

Quick-cooking cereal, such as oatmeal

Doughnuts—made in advance with a much richer egg and milk dough than standard on special order from a bakery, or homemade

Bread

Fruitcake in ration-size pieces. Use rich dough mixture on special order

Dried fruit, such as apricots, apples, etc.

Sugar

Coffee—instant or regular

Tea

Cocoa—dry-mix with sugar and dehydrated milk

Salt and personal choice of other seasoning

Where dogs are used for transportation, a supply of commercial or other dog food

Matches, best-grade wood, repacked into metal container

Toilet paper

Doughnuts should be frozen, and at every camp the next day's ration should be removed from the bulk stock, then thawed; and when about to leave for the trail in the morning, the daily doughnut ration should be put in a polyethylene bag and packed with the thermos bottle in a cloth drawstring bag that is insulated with down, pile, or layers of blanketing to prevent refreezing. The doughnuts will then be ready for the midmorning and midafternoon mug-up stops. Hot coffee, tea, or cocoa prepared in advance each day for the trail will be carried in thermos bottles, rather than stopping to heat water. Some heat does escape from hot filled thermos bottles, helping to keep the insulated doughnuts thawed.

Bread slices will freeze hard, and in this condition are not easily squashed. Nevertheless, bread should be protected in a grub box. Because of its porosity bread thaws very quickly in a warm camp or before an open fire. It can be toasted on top of the wood stove by sprinkling some salt on the stove to keep it from direct contact with the metal. Better yet, it will get an appetizing golden-brown toast color and flavor when browned in a hot, buttered frying pan. Outdoors, it can be impaled on a crotched stick held before an open fire.

Fruitcake, cut in individual-sized pieces, should be wrapped separately, or bagged in polyethylene. It is a very nourishing and a well-balanced food when it is made with generous proportions of nuts, fruit, eggs, milk, butter, sugar, etc. It is a food that also lends a bit of excitement to trail diet. For noon lunch, the fruitcake should be prethawed and kept with the thermos bottle of coffee, tea, or cocoa in the insulated bag, or in its polyethylene bag in a pocket under one's parka, where it will remain thawed by body heat.

Dried fruit is easily stewed, simply by adding water and setting it on the stove or over a campfire to cook until soft. No overnight soaking is necessary with some of the newer types. The cooking is usually done in the evening and the sauce consumed entirely for breakfast. Another method is to put the fruit in a wide-mouth thermos, pour boiling hot water into it, drain, then again pour in hot water and cork. By morning it is ready to eat. The first scald of hot water heats up the fruit and bottle liner, adding to the overnight heat.

Instant coffee has been so improved in recent times that for many people it satisfactorily replaces regular ground coffee. Ground coffee may be preferred. Its aroma is a strong argument in its favor.

Winter food is best separated into daily ration packets. A total of four to five pounds of food per day should be considered for each member of the party, where the meat portion is already prepared, or if the meat portion is fresh. Where meat is freeze-dried and other items are water-free, the weight can be cut to three pounds per man per day.

The list of provisions may seem limited in variety to the initiate, and excessively varied to those long on trail experience. It will, I am sure, be found more than ample where there is no pampering of appetites. None of the items listed will cause spoilage problems through deepfreezing and thawing on the trail.

The stewed meat, meatballs in gravy, and the baked beans, prepared ahead of the trip in frozen blocks and wrapped in waxed paper, rationed for each meal, require only thawing and heating.

Fresh meat will be precut, individually wrapped and rationed for each meal. It is not necessary, though better, to thaw meat before frying. For frozen steak, the fry pan should be partly covered, using a slow fire at the start until thawing is complete, then the heat should be stepped up for more rapid frying without a cover. Prethawing produces a better end result.

Bacon, separated into frozen slices and individually wrapped in waxed paper, need not be thawed before frying—simply unwrap, fry slowly, and turn often.

Scrambled, freeze-dried eggs need only the addition of hot water—no cooking. Hot water is added to the envelope in which a single individual portion is packed, the envelope shaken slightly, and the contents emptied onto a plate or eaten out of the envelope. They are as good as those scrambled by the individual cook from raw eggs. If weight permits, fresh eggs can be frozen hard and used in the regular way. Allow a short thawing of the shell, or dip the egg in hot water and shell it immediately. The icy chunk of egg will melt down in a frying pan and fry up as shapely as do the unfrozen eggs. For boiled eggs, place the frozen eggs in cold water and bring them to boil, continuing for either soft-or hard-boiled eggs.

An instant rice and a newly processed oatmeal need only the addition of hot water with no cooking, although I think you will prefer the three-minute variety better than the instant. Set aside for a short time after adding the hot water. See instructions on package. The instant oatmeal must be stirred after setting, but not the rice.

Hot cereals can be brought to a boil, placed in the wide-mouth thermos jar, and left overnight. The cereals will be well done for breakfast by the contained heat.

Instant mashed potatoes require the addition of dry milk, hot water, and a dab of butter to the dry potato product. It is then set aside for a minute and stirred briskly. Dry milk and salt can be added to the entire bulk instant potato supply before starting the trip. If potato patties are desired, prepare as for mashed potatoes, make into patties, dip in flour, and fry in bacon fat or butter. For hot potato soup, mix a combination of dry whole milk, instant potato, and celery salt in cold water, then heat. Add some regular salt if needed. Celery tops dried and pulverized by running them through a fine sieve are better than celery salt for potato soup. The amount of regular salt is then increased.

Dry whole milk for drinking purposes to be made more palatable should be reconstituted (mixed) several hours or more before consuming it. The morning cereal milk will be prepared the evening before and kept only near enough to the stove to prevent freezing.

Cocoa is made by combining dry whole milk, cocoa, sugar, and just a nip of salt. The imported Dutch cocoa has the finest flavor. These items in dry form should be mixed in bulk before the trip, or one can buy the standard prepared mix, though with some misgivings for richness. Simply add the cocoa mixture to hot water in a cup or pot, and stir. Add more dry milk to the dry cocoa mix for a better cocoa when using the commercial item.

One can usually fish through the ice and supplement the foregoing diet somewhat. Clean and scale the fish, or fillet it as soon as it is caught to avoid having to thaw the fish later before cleaning and scaling. Fish can be put into a fry pan frozen, covered until thawed out with a low heat, the cover then removed and the heat stepped up for frying. Be liberal with frying fat when frying fish. The fat can be stored in a friction top can and reused only for fish frying later. Frozen fish and meat placed in hot fat will spatter, so be careful of fat burns on face or hands. A cover used for the first few minutes of frying will avoid this hazard. Natives boil much of their fish. You can in time acquire a taste for it. Get the water boiling, add salt, then drop in the frozen fish. The fish will hold together better if you first put the pieces in a gauze bag and then drop the bag in the salted, boiling water.

INDEX

INDEX

Calvin Rutstrum (1895–1982) was one of the best-known outdoorsmen of his generation. During the 1960s, he enjoyed a wide following as interest in outdoor adventure boomed, and today he is recognized by canoe country aficionados who are fascinated by the lore of canoe travel and wilderness adventure. He is the author of more than a dozen books on wilderness travel and technique, including *The Wilderness Route Finder, The New Way of the Wilderness,* and *North American Canoe Country,* all published by the University of Minnesota Press.

www.ingramcontent.com/pod-product-compliance
Lightning Source LLC
LaVergne TN
LVHW090855210325
806483LV00004B/8